Dusty Miller's gentle, wise approach to women and men who distance from love offers a unique guide to finding real connection. This breakthough approach will change the lives of men and women who struggle with the challenges of intimacy.

—Terrence Real, director of the Relational Life Institute in Newton, MA, and author of the national best-sellers *I Don't Want to Talk About It* and *How Can I Get Through to You?*, as well as the recently published *New Rules of Marriage*

Stop Running from Love *offers a unique approach to problems of distance in intimate relationships. Miller's three-step model guides the reader to understand the past in order to revitalize existing relationships, and gently guides women and men to risk deeper connections in all their relationships.*

—Stephanie S. Covington, Ph.D., psychotherapist and author of *Leaving the Enchanted Forest* and *A Woman's Way Through the Twelve Steps*

Stop Running from Love

3 Steps to Overcoming Emotional Distancing & Fear of Intimacy

New Harbinger Publications, Inc.

Publisher's Note

This publication is designed to provide accurate and authoritative information in regard to the subject matter covered. It is sold with the understanding that the publisher is not engaged in rendering psychological, financial, legal, or other professional services. If expert assistance or counseling is needed, the services of a competent professional should be sought.

Distributed in Canada by Raincoast Books

New Harbinger Publications, Inc.
5674 Shattuck Avenue
Oakland, CA 94609
www.newharbinger.com

Cover design by Amy Shoup
Text design by Michele Waters-Kermes
Acquired by Melissa Kirk
Edited by Kayla Sussell

Printed in the United States of America

Library of Congress Cataloging-in-Publication Data

Miller, Dusty, 1944-
Stop running from love : overcome emotional distancing and fear of intimacy and embrace love in your life / Dusty Miller.
p. cm.
Includes bibliographical references.
ISBN-13: 978-1-57224-518-1 (pbk. : alk. paper)
ISBN-10: 1-57224-518-2 (pbk. : alk. paper)
1. Intimacy (Psychology) 2. Love. I. Title.
BF575.I5M53 2007
158.2--dc22

2007047451

10 09 08

10 9 8 7 6 5 4 3 2 1

First printing

Contents

Acknowledgments

I am grateful to my editors at New Harbinger Publications: Melissa Kirk for her ongoing enthusiasm and support for this project; Jess Beebe and Kayla Sussell for their creative, intelligent suggestions and improvements.

I could not have continued writing over the past few years without the compassionate friendship and vision of my agent, Susan Lee Cohen. Thanks, Susan, for your guidance and good company through the dry spells and floods of the past few years. Thanks also to my writing group brothers Jonathan Diamond and Roget Lockhard whose faith and good humor kept me chugging along.

To those who have participated in the distancer dance with me—you know who you are—thank you for all I have learned from you, and thanks to Laura Curran for the "group."

Thanks to Marcelle and Tim Morgan for showing me how the generosity of your love for each other and for your family extends many life-giving roots and branches, and to Savanna Ouellette and Katie Tolles, whose power of example makes me believe in lasting partnerships.

Introduction: Meet the Distancer

Distancers. Who are they? What are they? They are men and women. They are those who completely avoid romantic relationships, or those who keep their partners at an emotional arm's length. They can be young, middle-aged, or old. They may either end their romantic relationships when things start getting serious, or they keep changing partners, looking for the perfect mate. Many distancers are in committed relationships but they still distance themselves from their partners emotionally or sexually. Some distancers make themselves too busy with work, family, friends, or activities to be available to their partner. But in spite of their many forms, all distancers have two things in common: they all have a great longing for intimacy and an equally great fear of intimacy.

If you are wondering whether you might be a distancer, try answering the questions on the following page.

Test Yourself

- Are you lonely or dissatisfied even though you're in a couple relationship?
- Do you feel there's a wall between your partner and yourself?
- Do you often move toward a new love but then run away?
- Does your relationship with food, drugs, work, or your computer feel more important to you than a relationship with another human being?
- Do you have trouble opening up emotionally or sexually?
- Have all your friends found partners while you are still wondering when your soul mate will show up?

If you answered yes to any of the above questions, then this book is for you!

Deep down, most of us continue to hope for and believe in a lasting love. There is no single theory to explain why this is so, but the desire for love seems to be basic to human nature. Love transcends the biological need to have sex or the economic motive to team up to run the family farm or business. For most people, it would seem that love is a force more powerful even than greed or envy. Whether we choose love or it chooses us, we incorporate it into our physical, mental, emotional, and spiritual life and value it as among the most precious conditions of being human.

For better or for worse, we might as well learn to make the best of it.

My Story

Like a multitude of other men and women, I felt desire for something I could not name. It took me a long time to understand that when it came to couple relationships, I was a distancer. I was astonished when

I finally realized that I had been distancing myself from love for a long, long time.

I knew that my close relationships had been affected by the childhood abuse I had experienced. Wise teachers, compassionate therapists, and loving friends had helped me analyze how the betrayals of my childhood had shaped me. But it took a long time for me to learn who I really was in a couple relationship. I didn't want to face the truth: my childhood experiences had caused me to distance myself mentally, physically, emotionally, and spiritually from genuine closeness with intimate companions.

It took the loss of several potentially golden opportunities before I could finally recognize and acknowledge that I kept my partners at a distance. Even though I understood that childhood violations and betrayals had had a powerful impact on my ability to form close relationships, insight alone could not help me change. I danced away from lasting love, protecting myself from opening up and risking the vulnerability of deep connection. I had many close friends and a series of loving partners, but I was lonely. I wanted to escape the pervasive sense of loneliness I felt, but I didn't know how. I became increasingly despairing about the hand that life had dealt me, doubting that I would ever experience genuine openness and trust.

When I became a psychotherapist, I had wanted to help others who had similar emotional scars caused by fear, betrayal, and mistrust. I had been taught to align myself with the "pursuer" in the couple, that is, the person who had the most invested in making the relationship work. Because women were usually the ones who sought professional help for the couple, they were viewed as the pursuers. So my job was to help the woman to skillfully negotiate the pitfalls of love, to accept that she needed to gently maneuver her partner without appearing to push him. Although I had my doubts about it always being the woman's responsibility to coax the uncommunicative male partner out of his cave, I hadn't yet fully understood that women could be distancers too. I certainly had not yet identified myself as a distancer.

Perhaps the most helpful lesson I learned when working with couples was to involve their families, friends, and community, no matter which half of the couple was distancing her- or himself from love. My experience taught me that it really does "take a village" to help transform couple relationships and to guide those who are still searching for love. It was through my own involvement in various forms of community that I was finally able to recognize and begin to change my own distancer identity.

You Are Not Alone

Perhaps, like me, you've tried for a long time to ignore the longing deep within you, the small voice that tells you you're missing out on something essential to your happiness. Maybe you've pushed your disappointments so far back into your unconscious mind that you barely know you are lonely. Perhaps you've tried to put your past behind you and move on, yet you keep wondering why there's still an invisible wall between you and your partner or why the partner you're still hoping to find hasn't appeared yet.

Maybe you are someone who reads everything you can find about love and intimacy. Maybe you've tried to figure out how to make love work through the advice of therapists, friends, even talk shows. And yet, in spite of all the searching that you've been doing, you are still feeling shut down or unsatisfied in some deep place. You may have assumed that the problem was your partner's inability to get to a deeper level of intimacy.

Love's landscape can open up for you—trust me on this. Something compelled you to pick up this book. Something within you wanted to explore the story of the distancer. You are willing to try something new, and that's all you need—willingness, and a map of the territory you are about to explore. You will discover that you can leave loneliness behind, and become a successful participant in satisfying, lasting, joyful relationships. You are fully capable of becoming more connected and emotionally open without risking total heartbreak. I know. This is my story too.

Risking Hope

Even with the promise that you can survive the vulnerability of opening to love, you may feel skeptical about trying something new. You may believe there's nothing new for you to learn about finding and keeping the love and intimacy you want. Here's why reading this book will provide you with something you aren't likely to have encountered before:

- You will learn to identify a broad spectrum of distancing styles and relationship scenarios. You will not have to choose a fixed identity or label. You won't have to decide whether you are love-addicted or love-avoidant. You don't even have to make a definitive decision about whether you're a distancer or a pursuer.

- You will discover there is a variety of distancer profiles. For example, you may identify as a distancer who stays within the couple relationship. Or maybe you'll recognize yourself as someone who creates distance by keeping one foot out the door. Perhaps you'll find yourself among the distancers who completely avoid couple relationships.

- You will learn that, in some relationships, you may be more likely to be vulnerable, open, and committed than you are in others.

- You are likely to see yourself as having been in different places along the distancing spectrum depending on the various relationships you've had. Or you may distance yourself more or less depending on the different stages of the same relationship.

- You won't have to be typecast by gender. Buying into gender stereotypes can cause women and men to become seriously disconnected in their couple relationships, without ever getting to the root of their unhappiness. Oversimplified assumptions about gender differences disempower both men and women.

- Whether you are a male or a female distancer, you may find it liberating to discover that there are many women who are distancers. Men who are labeled "commitment phobic" or "love-avoidant" are caught in the glare of floodlights while

> women who distance get lost in the shadows. Just as it took a long time to become public knowledge that men as well as women can be victims of childhood abuse and violence, so too it has been long overlooked that both men and women distance themselves from intimacy.

Women and men both yearn for intimacy and deeper connection, and both genders can create disabling distancing patterns in their couple relationships. Without adequate information to help them name, tame, and transform the runaway self, both male and female distancers often convince themselves that the love they have is as good as it's going to get. You will learn that it takes a village to create a healthy couple relationship. One of the major mistakes in trying to solve intimacy problems happens when the focus is exclusively on the couple. No couple is ever really alone on a desert island. Too often, everyone tries to fix the couple as if they exist in isolation. Friends, family, and helping professionals often fail to give enough attention to the importance of the big picture. There are many ways that a couple is a part of their "village."

You will learn how to integrate all the aspects of community that help to create and nurture a healthy couple. You will also learn the importance of your own social and cultural roots, the significance of religious or spiritual communities, and the value of workplaces, extended families, neighborhoods, friendship networks, and the larger geographical community.

How It Works: Creating Change

Here is a preview of how the work we will do together will guide you through this new journey away from loneliness. In this book we will be using a three-step approach called the ARC model. ARC is an abbreviation for Awareness, Remembering, and Connecting.

Step One: Awareness

The first step involves developing your awareness about the many ways that people distance. You will be given the necessary tools and questionnaires to help you identify how you see yourself in a couple, and you'll read about a variety of other distancers so that you can locate yourself—or someone you care for—among the profiles of distancers.

You will begin doing the first step by learning about the most common forms of distancing. A series of exercises in Step One will help you relate your own patterns of distancing to the examples of other distancers. You will also be guided to see the strengths within your vulnerabilities. Awareness becomes transforming only when you understand and honor your strengths and gifts in addition to those difficult areas that need to change.

Step Two: Remembering

Going back to the roots of how you have developed your beliefs, fears, and hopes about intimate relationships can be both very exciting and illuminating. It can also stir up old memories and emotions that many distancers would prefer to avoid. The ARC model is based in a strong commitment to safety, so you will be guided very carefully through the process of remembering. The goal is not to go backwards to relive old painful experiences, but to examine your formative relationships to study how they shaped you to become the person you are.

You will trace the various influences that combined to create your distancer patterns. You will, of course, be examining the close relationships you had in the family you grew up in. You'll also review the prevailing beliefs about love and intimacy at the time you grew up, and how your cultural roots shaped you. That is, you will look at your race, ethnicity, class, geographical home, neighborhood, religion, schooling, and even how the media influenced you. You will also take a good look at the relationships you've experienced in your adult life to see how your fears, hopes, longings, and even aversions have been determined.

Step Three: Connection

The third step moves you into the action phase. This step will guide you to begin developing your abilities to create many levels of deepening connection. You will begin to target the changes you may feel ready to undertake. You will practice new activities and ways of thinking that will gradually help you to experience deeper connections with others. The way we will approach change involves a gentle, gradual process of engaging with others at a new level of intimacy. This work allows the wary distancer to proceed at a safe pace while avoiding slipping back into the all-too-familiar patterns of running and hiding.

In Step Three, you will try out new skills that will help you to make good connections with others in a variety of settings. You'll practice new skills in your friendships, at your workplace, in support groups and other communities, and new skills for relating to your family, both the one you grew up in, and, when relevant, your current family.

You will also learn how to revitalize and make new connections in the various communities that support you and your partner (or potential partner). This could mean getting involved in new recreational activities, participating more actively in groups that make a difference in the well-being of others, finding a community that supports you spiritually, engaging more completely in support groups, or joining with other parents to make a better life for your children (if that is relevant). Or perhaps you may want to go back to school or engage in other learning experiences that will allow you to connect in new ways.

Finally, you will practice new ways of connecting with your current partner or someone with whom you might just be starting a relationship. These activities and exercises will offer gentle, nonthreatening ways to make changes in your approach to intimate relationships. If you are single, you will learn new ways to approach potential significant others. You are going to change your way of approaching intimacy at exactly the right pace for yourself. You will know intuitively when to push yourself and when to slow down. You will learn to trust yourself to make the best changes for yourself at the right pace and with the right people.

Each of the three steps requires a commitment to becoming focused and trying out something new. The information and exercises in this book will help you create a solid foundation for freedom and joy in your intimate relationships. Of course, no real transformation can take place without some hard work. Insight may happen in a sudden flash, but transformation takes both inspiration and perspiration.

The good news is that you don't have to do it alone. In the following chapters, you will learn how to engage in each step and you will learn how others have used the ARC model to leave loneliness behind.

Learning from Other Distancers

In this book, you'll have the opportunity to follow the stories of a variety of distancers. You will learn how they used distancing, where their distancing got started, and how they were able to transform and transcend their distancing patterns. There are many reasons to share these stories. Healing generally works best through a process of identification that allows you to see parts of yourself in another person's experience. These stories will also provide you with a connection to a community of other people who have struggled with the same issues you are facing. By becoming acquainted with the distancers in this book, you will not have to make the major changes you plan to make in isolation.

As you begin the process of engaging with this new model of change, you'll be provided with many opportunities to explore all of the interrelated influences that contribute to becoming a distancer. You will undoubtedly find stories quite similar to your own and stories that are very different. This approach emphasizes understanding the larger context of what made us who we are and teaches us how to change our intimate relationships by making deeper connections in our communities.

Instead of trying to understand and change everything having to do with your intimate relationships, you will begin your journey by entering the community of women and men who are also accomplished distancers through hearing their stories. By doing this, you will learn how to make deeper connections within the "village" that is needed to support every couple's health and happiness.

The Willingness to Say Yes

For readers who are willing to open to intimacy in love, the information and exercises in this book will lead to change. Of course, when you recognize how you've been sabotaging your relationships, you will have to risk opening yourself to vulnerability and possible heartbreak. So if you've chosen to look at the distancing factors in how you relate to intimates, you are taking a brave step.

Safe Passage Through Love's Landscape

You are now entering exciting new territory where you are, indeed, the expert.

When you identify yourself as a distancer, you take the first step toward change. Beginning your safe passage through the threatening terrain of intimacy may often be uncomfortable. However, this book will help you to move slowly and it will allow you to give yourself lots of wiggle room. Reassure yourself that if this is not the right time for you to make big changes, you can stay right where you are until you feel ready.

Most distancers resist giving up the defenses that have allowed them to feel safe, even though they may have endured years of dissatisfaction and loneliness. My approach to working with distancers is to begin one step removed from any major change-making interactions. In my years of working with traumatized children and adults, I've learned that change often needs to be a slow, gentle process, emphasizing recovery through mindfulness of the mind-body connection. Too often the distancer is threatened by confrontational statements or advised to change behaviors that have functioned as protection against loss or pain. It is obvious that forcing the distancer to try something that feels too threatening will only increase the distancer's need to run or put up a wall.

Using the Mind-Body Connection

Everyone needs a variety of learning modalities to approach old problems; variety in how you can learn will help you to access parts of your brain you haven't used before. You will not only learn more about your communication and choice-making patterns, but you will be offered exercises to help you become aware of how your body tells its own story and creates warning signals and roadblocks, as well as opening new doors to change.

All of the work you are about to begin will help you move into closer relationships by teaching you to use mindfulness, to surrender control over the things that have kept you in a defensive place up until now. You will learn to feel comfortable with the idea that you do not actually have very much control over others or many of the circumstances that come your way. This is a process that involves a new awareness of old patterns that have been operating under the radar for a long time. It draws on new research and intervention tactics based in twenty-first-century knowledge of how our complex brains work in close relationships.

The Freedom to Say No

There is no rule that says all human beings must be in deep, committed relationships. This book may help you become comfortable with remaining single (or supporting someone else in that choice). Some people recognize that they are neither lonely nor unhappy being single, despite the social pressure to form couple relationships. Many single people have satisfying lives filled with friends, work, creativity, spiritual pursuits, and so forth, and do not experience chronic unhappiness or loneliness.

How to Use This Book

You will need a notebook or journal to write in (or you can take notes on your computer) as you work through the exercises in this book. You are beginning the process of creating your own book, one in which you're the expert about yourself, something you can look over periodically to see how far you have come, while you move along your path to healthier relationships. You will be guided to write down your answers to the questions and to make notes so you won't forget your initial responses to what you will have just read. It's common for people to quickly forget something that makes them nervous or uncomfortable. Recording your thoughts and discoveries is a very important part of the change process. The odds are good that if you simply read this book without actively engaging in its exercises, you will miss valuable clues for solving the mysteries of your relational life.

You Can Do It!

This is the moment to take a true leap of faith and to give yourself another chance. Love may not be easy, but when it works, it's worth the journey.

Through many years as a psychotherapist and as a survivor, I've learned how the human spirit can transcend old forms of bondage. Today, distancing is a growing challenge for both women and men in their intimate relationships. I've been inspired by my work with people trapped in the aftermath of traumatic experiences. I've witnessed the many ways traumatized people sabotage their relationships but eventually learn to love and be loved. I have a deep and genuine optimism that we can learn to hold our ground and stay steady on the path of love.

All distancers have the capacity to end the dissatisfaction that shrouds their relationships. Despite your disappointments in love, you are now risking hope. Somewhere deep inside yourself, you've always believed that your loneliness will end, that your relationship problems eventually will become something you will have the tools to fix. If you are ready to embark on an ultimately successful journey through the slippery slopes of love, this book can offer you a new perspective on relationships and it will teach you effective strategies for change.

This book may be helpful even if you don't identify yourself as a distancer. You can share what you learn from the book with a partner or friend who is a distancer. Or perhaps the people you get involved with are distancers, and this book will help you understand them better. You may work in a professional role with people who distance. Whatever your experience, you will benefit from exploring this new, uncharted territory. You may even surprise yourself by getting acquainted with the distancer part of yourself.

Take this opportunity to feel the freshness of starting a new chapter in your life—even if right now there's no significant other in your heart. Keep yourself open and willing, trust that you will stay firm on solid ground, and let yourself enjoy your journey to true intimacy.

1 Recognizing Yourself

When you name something, you begin the process of making a connection. A new pet becomes part of your family from the moment you give it a name. Once we can identify an illness, we know how to treat its symptoms. You can begin to leave loneliness behind by identifying yourself (or someone you care about) along the distancer spectrum.

You may have recognized that something is missing in your experience of intimate relationships, but you don't really know how to identify your relationship dilemmas. You will probably feel both curiosity and anxiety as you discover new ways to name that impenetrable cloud that comes between you and others. You will feel less alone when you can identify with other people who also maintain a whirlwind of activity between themselves and others, or who pull back, run away, or hide from intimacy.

In this chapter you'll be introduced to the various ways that people distance in their romantic relationships. Reading the stories of others who distance in or from their relationships will help you learn to identify the ways that you are a distancer. You will begin with some thinking and writing about yourself, using various exercises to help you deepen and expand your knowledge of yourself.

To start this new venture, look for yourself among the following styles of distancing.

The Many Faces of the Distancer

"Distancing" is a big category. Distancers come in many shapes and sizes. They can be single or in long-term couple relationships, gay or straight, women or men, young or old. Here are a few brief glimpses of typical distancers:

Typical Distancing Patterns

The sexual distancer. Yvonne dreads the weekends. Her partner will want to make love and Yvonne will find herself once again coming up with an excuse or else just leaving her body during the love-making. "I can feel love, but I can't open myself up sexually," she writes in her journal.

Yvonne is a sexual distancer.

The emotional distancer. Howard is married to a distancer. He tells the marriage counselor, "I know that Sally cares about me, but she just never has time for me. It's the kids, it's her best friend calling up in the middle of some big drama, it's a deadline at work—you name it and she's got it." If a couple needed attention like a person needs food, this couple here would have starved to death a long time ago.

Howard's wife, Sally, is a "Superwoman" distancer, keeping herself distracted from intimacy by all the things she does for others. Men also engage in this form of distancing, often as workaholics, sports addicts, or Superdads who have no time for their partners.

Chris is another emotional distancer. Beth complains about Chris, who is her partner, this way: "I just can't get through to her," she says, with a weary shrug of her shoulders. "It feels a lot of the time like there's nobody home emotionally." Beth doesn't want to leave Chris—they've been together for ten years. But she does want a deeper emotional connection.

The controlling distancer. Rick is a thirty-something married man with two children. He is a big, powerful guy who was a football star in high school. He married Carla, his high school girlfriend, right after he completed two years of military service. Rick distances by being so completely in charge of everything that Carla equates their marriage to living in a perpetual boot camp, with Rick always barking orders at her and the kids. Now that their older son has hit adolescence, he is starting to rebel against his father's military style of parenting. Rick's efforts to take care of everything and everyone around him have led the couple to the brink of divorce.

Rick distances by being a control freak.

Mutual distancing. Jack and Diane are both distancers. Diane began breaking up with Jack not long after they began their love-at-first-sight steamy romance. "I'm really sorry, but I don't think I'm ready to get into anything serious right now," she tells him. "I know, I know… I said that you were everything I ever wanted and I never wanted us to be apart. I'm really sorry, but I've realized I need to take some time for myself. I'll call you…"

Diane will, in fact, call Jack. She will cajole him to come back before he's even finished the two-hour drive back to Connecticut where he lives. This drama will be played out many times before Jack realizes that he has to be the one to walk away.

Diane is a very fearful distancer. She has a history of falling in love, but then changing her mind. Jack is a distancer too, but he always ends up looking like the "good guy." Jack distances by using high levels of denial, shutting down inside, and never recognizing his complicity in their mutual distancing dance.

The ambivalent distancer. Ben's friends are talking about whether they should invite him over to meet their recently divorced friend Jill. "You know, I'd hate to see Jill get her hopes up…" Molly says to her husband.

"Ben will just do what he always does. Start out as Mr. Wonderful and then eventually it will be 'Hi Ho Silver Away!' Jill won't know what hit her."

Ben typifies the kind of ambivalent distancer who is great at the beginning of a relationship. Unfortunately, he always finds a good reason to back away when the relationship starts to get serious.

Varieties of avoidant distancers. Danny is another charming distancer with a slightly different operating style. He has been dating the same woman for three years, but keeps himself locked away in a mental fortress populated with fantasy characters. He is a successful young science-fiction writer, but he is afraid to enter the real world of the heart.

Janine has a great time with her friends, but she avoids intimate relationships completely. She is resistant when anyone tries to get her to meet a man. She says she's "not interested." Yet Janine secretly hopes that one day the right man will magically step into her world. Janine is the classic "someday my prince will come" distancer, terrified of being vulnerable, yet hoping The One will show up and magically make love feel safe for her.

Andrew is like Janine—he's a distancer who can't get close enough to a potential partner to establish a relationship. He can't slow down long enough to make it through an entire evening, let alone a lasting relationship. Andrew spins through life, a charming, desirable young man who wants an intimate relationship but has no idea how he can make that happen.

Andrew and Janine are both examples of distancers who seem to be relationship phobic and yet long to find love.

Distancer Categories

There are three broad and encompassing distancer categories: the *Disappearing Distancer*, the *Defended Distancer*, and the *Distracted Distancer*. Within each of these categories, there are predictable variations. The people you've just met fit into these categories and illustrate variations within these three central divisions.

The Disappearing Distancer

Disappearing distancers are the easiest category of distancers to identify. You may recognize yourself as the disappearing distancer who completely avoids getting into relationships. Or you may be the type of disappearing distancer who occasionally approaches courtship but is too afraid of being trapped or smothered to stick around for long.

The Defended Distancer

The second category is crowded, so if you are a defended distancer you have plenty of company. The defended distancer gets into relationships but always has one foot out the door or seems to float in and out of relational reach. Sometimes, the defended distancer is a perfectionist, unable to settle for a "good enough" relationship, even when it's right there at the doorstep. This is just another way to avoid feeling vulnerable: "I'll reject you before you can reject or abandon me."

The defended distancer is more covert in his or her distancing behavior than the disappearing distancer, but is also fearful about risking emotional and/or sexual vulnerability. Defended distancers are often tortured by their ambivalence, never allowing themselves to feel securely attached in their relationships. Upsetting themselves and their partners, they change their minds back and forth, first in, then out.

Much of what we know about gender stereotypes would make us think that most defended distancers are men. But if you are a woman who avoids emotional vulnerability, you aren't alone. Many women keep themselves emotionally at a distance. They are less likely to be confronted about it, though. One obvious reason for this is that most men have been socialized to avoid emotional vulnerability and so the male partners of female distancers may not easily recognize what's really going on. Also, female emotional distancing is underreported in books, magazines, research studies, and frequently goes undetected in couples counseling.

The Distracted Distancer

The third category is the best disguised among the three major categories of distancer. The distracted distancer appears in many manifestations. The distracted distancer stays too busy to spend quality time with her (or his) partner, thus avoiding couple closeness and intimacy. Distracted distancers may be superproviders, focusing all their efforts on accomplishing necessary tasks: parenting, working, keeping up the home, doing community service, and so on. When the distracted distancer's efforts are on behalf of the family, he or she can appear to be very committed to the well-being of the partner, even though the couple relationship is getting shortchanged.

There are many different manifestations of the distracted distancer. One example is the crisis addict who is swept up in one crisis after another, leaving little time or space for anything else. Someone who is involved in an all-consuming spiritual practice, or is a full-time advocate for the homeless, or has dedicated his or her life to protecting the environment is likely to have a partner who feels neglected by this distracted distancer.

Celia, Super Businesswoman

Celia runs her own real estate business. She's an attractive woman who hopes she'll find the partner of her dreams. Her marriage ended in divorce. Her husband had an affair that left Celia shaken and vulnerable, but she has dated on and off for quite a while. She is puzzled by her ongoing single life. "Why can't I find someone?" she asks her therapist.

The answer lies in Celia's total focus on her career. She works at least fifty hours a week, leaving herself almost no time to meet potential partners or to deepen a new relationship.

"What happened to that nice guy you had dinner with?" Celia's sister asks.

Celia shakes her head. "I'm not really sure," she admits. "We were having a great time kind of joking around online. It seemed like it was hard to find a time to get together. I guess I don't really know what happened."

Like other distracted distancers, Celia avoids getting hurt again by keeping a whirlwind of activity between herself and her potential love interests. She is so busy that she scarcely notices that her dates eventually give up after discovering how difficult it is to spend time with her.

How to Work with the Exercises

As you read through the descriptions of the following distancing styles, you may discover that you also recognize yourself in these descriptions. Keep track of all that you discover about yourself by working with the questionnaires. Make notes at the end of each section so that you can contrast and compare your own experiences with what you've read at the end of the chapter. Everything you write will help you focus on what seems to fit your style most significantly and will direct you to the changes you will be making as we move from Step One to Step Three.

Exercise

Finding the Distancer Description That Fits You

This is the first of many exercises designed to help you find yourself, and give you the tools you need to help in analyzing and eventually changing your distancer patterns. This is the time you should start the journal discussed in the introduction.

Take a few minutes right now to write down whatever first impressions come to you about the distancing styles you've been reading about.

If you have trouble starting to write, you can begin by answering these questions: Whom do you most identify with? Do you think you have a little bit of each distancing style in your repertoire? Has your distancing style changed over time?

Even if you just write only a few sentences, it will help you begin to keep a record of your developing awareness about the distancing you do in your relationships.

Learning from Stories About Distancers

Now that you've got an overview of the territory, you are ready to jump in, and learn from the following stories about these various distancers. This will give you more information about how other people enact their distancing patterns. Just like listening to someone's story on a talk show or in a support group, reading about other distancers will help you to learn more about yourself. It will also help you to feel a connection with others who've been struggling with the same feelings of bewilderment and loneliness.

Be aware that as you begin to recognize yourself as a distancer, you may feel shaken by this new identity. But keep in mind that the self you are beginning to discover is not a one-dimensional cartoon character. Don't go to extremes: nothing is ever as simple and one-dimensional as the daily horoscopes in the newspaper would have us believe. You've always been a complex person, you've always varied in how you relate to others in the different parts of your life. You are now just beginning to explore new parts of yourself: nothing should be written in stone.

Here's another cautionary note: distancers are not always consistent in their relationships. You can be a major distancer in one relationship, but less so in another. Or, as your life or your partners change, you may utilize different styles of distancing. You may discover that more than one of the distancer styles fit you. What's important is to begin to learn about yourself using these profiles as a point of reference. No one size fits all and no one remains the same size forever.

The Disappearing Distancer

The disappearing distancer is the person who avoids intimate relationships, exhibiting a relational form of anorexia. This kind of distancer, consciously or not, wishes for an intimate relationship yet avoids allowing this to develop.

The disappearing distancer usually avoids intimate relationships in order to decrease the risk of dependency and possible emotional devastation. Like every other form of distancing, the disappearing distancer uses distancing as a survival tool by trying to defend against painful loss, rejection, or exploitation. Because of keeping potential partners at a distance, the disappearing distancer may be deeply lonely. She may not know this at a conscious level, telling herself that instead of enduring the hassles that come with a relationship, she is choosing creativity, a brilliant career, dedication to her spiritual practice, or getting to know herself as a single, unencumbered person. But unlike the person who is genuinely content and committed to being single, the disappearing distancer harbors fantasies of being in a happy couple.

The Distancer Who Fears Herself

Sometimes the most virulent force behind the avoidant patterns of the disappearing distancer is the fear of being consumed by her (or his) own desires or needs.

Julie's Story

Julie is a college student who is terrified by her own hunger for connection. One morning while we were walking in the woods behind my house, she described her fear of engulfing others. She told me, "I sometimes think… I don't know how to say this, but I think I could just gulp down any person I started to like. Just, like, gobble him up, you know?" It's a beautiful day, but Julie doesn't seem to notice the brilliant colors of the leaves on the path as she scuffs along beside me.

I glanced at my unhappy young companion. She is lovely, although her short buzz haircut and many piercings challenge my fashion sense. Like many other women of her generation, tattoos, multiple earrings, and big shoes are her cultural statements, but beneath her in-your-face style is the soft vulnerability of a runaway bunny. I was wearing a long-sleeved jersey and jeans for our walk, while Julie wore a skintight sleeveless T-shirt. She clumped along in her heavy boots, oddly graceful in her long, flowing cotton skirt decorated with colorful embroidery and tiny mirrors.

Julie grew up in a family where there was good reason to be afraid of swallowing someone whole. Her mother suffered from severe depression. Julie has become increasingly horrified by the idea that she could be just like her mother, a woman whose terrible needs threatened to devour her daughter. Julie was afraid she would never escape her mother's hunger.

"I never invited other kids over to my house," she told me. "I never knew if my mother would be friendly or if she would start crying in front of them and tell us to go outside so she could go back to sleep. The kids knew there was something wrong with her, so they didn't really want to come to my house anyway." Over time, the shame Julie felt about her mother took her over so completely that she developed a pervasive sense of shame about herself.

Julie is already practiced in the self-sabotaging patterns of distancing even though she is only nineteen years old. Although her behavior is not yet at the extreme end of the spectrum, she is driven to keep herself at an impenetrable distance from others. She was quick to tell me that it's safer to run away from others rather than face her own hungry ghosts. She hides from anyone who might become a potential partner. She said, "Sometimes, people tell me I'm weird. Some of the kids in my dorm even call me 'The Mystery Girl.'"

Julie illustrates the disappearing distancer who suffers from fear, shame, and self-loathing, feelings that have propelled her into hiding.

The Isolated Distancer

Spending a great deal of your time alone becomes self-sabotaging when it keeps you from recognizing, deepening, and enjoying human connection. The habit of being alone, when generated by negative feelings toward others, can become a chronic condition of isolation. Feeling driven to back away from others is often based on shame.

Isolation, in and of itself, is a by-product of distancing that creates its own problems. In the prison system, being placed in solitary confinement has always been the gravest of punishments. When people put themselves into their own prison of isolation, they lose confidence in their rightful place in human society. Feeling perpetually outside of life can cause you to feel rejected and defective. Over time, you may become increasingly fearful, resentful, anxious, depressed, or angry.

Isolation is self-perpetuating. It is potentially lethal when it leads to extremes of depression and hopelessness and can take someone to the point of suicide. Someone like Julie, who never seems to initiate contact with others, is perceived as aloof, arrogant, or unfriendly. This in turn creates feelings of loneliness and defensiveness.

Andrew's Story

Andrew was an appealing but elusive client who popped in and out of my therapy practice at erratic intervals. He told me that he had come to therapy because he really wanted a partner, but he couldn't seem to get anything started. When I asked Andrew if he was committed to doing the work it would take for him to find a partner, he was enthusiastic. "You got it! I'm going to be here, no fear. Definitely! I'm going to make it to every appointment this month and the next and the next. You've got my word."

However, as a rule, long before the hour was over, he sailed out of my office, whistling and humming cheerfully, and greeting anyone who happened to be in the waiting room.

Inevitably, Andrew failed to stick to the schedule. During the first few months with me, he missed many appointments. When we did meet, his ability to pay attention was too scattered for him to be able to focus on his distancing patterns. We weren't making much progress in helping him to identify the specific ways he distanced, although I was beginning to spot his pattern. It was hard to help Andrew to focus because of his speedy monologues and his lightning-quick exits before we had settled into a topic.

Andrew was a complex person who very rarely felt comfortable inside his own skin. Generally, he was tormented by being unable to stick to any given plan. He couldn't follow through, whether it was a plan to move to another part of the country or go back to school, or even just a plan to get a cup of coffee with a friend. He was reluctant to make choices, from something as small as choosing what movie to see, to something more significant like signing a lease for an apartment or getting a full-time job. Because of his across-the-board style of restlessness and avoidance, Andrew couldn't even get close to starting an intimate relationship.

Like many other distancers I have known, Andrew had a history of drug and alcohol dependence, but, miraculously, considering his restless style, he had been able to stay clean for ten years. He attended a 12-step meeting almost every day, but could rarely make it through the entire hour. Yet despite his extreme restlessness, he remained determined to stay clean and sober. Most of his siblings were in various stages of physical and economic failure because of their active addictions. Andrew's mother desperately wanted more for her youngest son, and her support was the foundation of Andrew's tenuous abstinence. Being involved in 12-step programs was his only successful effort at risking connection. I understood this single area of success: it felt safe because Andrew was relating to an entire group rather than allowing himself to be vulnerable with one person.

When I asked Andrew to describe what it was like for him to sit with me in therapy and try to talk about himself, he described extreme mental restlessness. He gave me a quick sketch of his internal and external process whenever he was alone with one other person. He said he couldn't concentrate on the other person, changing his mind every few minutes about what he wanted to do next, or thinking about someone or something else, instead of staying focused in the present moment. As soon as he settled down physically, he would begin to think of something else he should be doing instead. Because of his extreme agitation and trouble with committing to the moment, he would precipitously leave whatever he was supposed to be doing, abandoning people even in his casual *encounters such as coffee dates with friends. As you might imagine, his attempts to date were disastrous.*

"My AA sponsor said to keep telling me 'be here now' but I just couldn't do it," Andrew confessed. Although it seemed clear that he was suffering from attention-deficit disorder and extreme anxiety, the support provided by medication and anxiety-focused behavioral modification therapy did not seem to help him approach intimacy with a partner.

As I got to know Andrew better, I began to understand that despite his hyperactive avoidance patterns, he had a lot going for him. He was an optimistic, loving person who sincerely wanted to find relief from the self-sabotaging behavior that kept him running in circles. He was capable of changing, but not until he was ready to understand how his distancing style controlled his life. It would require both willingness and openness to new insights and new activities before he would be able to take his first step in successfully challenging his relationship problems.

Janine's Story

Janine, a baby-faced blonde in her late twenties, was a participant in one of my trauma and addiction recovery groups. Like many other disappearing distancers, Janine habitually spent much of her time alone. She was fearful of others and she suffered intense shame about her experience of having been victimized.

At nineteen, Janine had been sexually assaulted by several men she met at a bar. After her traumatic efforts to disclose the rape, she grew increasingly silent and withdrawn. Her friends and family either doubted her story or blamed her for the assault. It was even suggested that she had been at fault because she had been partying like everyone else at the bar.

When she first met with a counselor she disclosed the details of the rape, but she had already given up trying to explain her complex and painful reactions to the entire traumatic experience, including the sense of betrayal she'd felt when those close to her blamed her. She had made up her mind to trust no one and built a fortress around her body and spirit; the main foundation of her fortress was her addictive overeating.

When Janine's weight gain became a potential threat to her health, a friend suggested she should try going to the nearby women's community resource center where she could participate in a free exercise and nutrition program. It was there that she became willing to join one of my recovery groups, encouraged by the stories of other women who were regulars at the center. She became willing to try again, knowing that she would be with others who shared her experience of violation and shame.

Before Janine came to the women's center, she had stopped going out at all. She ordered take-out deliveries and got her sister to shop for her other necessities. She did not use her time alone in pursuits that satisfied her. She was trapped in a prison of isolation by the shame and hopelessness of feeling damaged beyond repair. Until Janine found a way to begin trusting others in the group, she had been the victim of her self-imposed isolation. Later, she would take on the challenge of moving toward an intimate relationship.

Exercise

Are You a Disappearing Distancer?

Here is a simple exercise to help you compare your behavior with this style of distancing. Use the following scale to rank yourself:

1 = This doesn't describe me at all.
2 = This describes my behavior a little bit.
3 = This describes my behavior in some ways.
4 = This describes quite a lot of my behavior.
5 = This is definitely me.

Now, read the following statements and rate each answer from 1 to 5.

Scores

1. I prefer being by myself in almost all circumstances. ______
2. I don't initiate social activities with others, that is, I don't ask other people out for coffee or start conversations with people I'm sitting next to at social gatherings. ______
3. I prefer the company of animals to people because you don't have to talk. ______
4. I don't mind meeting new people but I don't pursue trying to get to know them better. ______
5. I don't mind being in a group as long as I don't have to get involved in one-on-one conversations. ______
6. I think that if anyone really got to know me well, he (or she) would probably be freaked out by me. ______
7. I don't let anyone get too close because they could end up wanting too much. ______
8. I don't understand what people find to just chitchat about. I don't feel comfortable discussing my life on such a superficial level. ______
9. I can relax only by doing things alone, like walking, watching TV, reading, and so forth. ______
10. I would want to be in a couple only if the other person was a lot like me and didn't expect me to keep up all that closeness and sharing. ______

Now, add up your total score. **Total Score** ______

If your score was under 35, that means this category doesn't describe you.

If your score was between 45 and 50, then you are very likely to be a disappearing distancer.

If you scored somewhere between 35 and 45, there are definitely some aspects of the disappearing distancer that fit your relational style.

Use the information you just obtained from answering this questionnaire to make a few notes about yourself in your journal. Notice which aspects of the disappearing distancer seem to resonate most strongly with your experience of yourself. Note whether there are some things you feel okay about and don't plan to change. Notice what upsets you the most. Which things would you most like to change?

The Defended Distancer

The second category of distancing includes women and men who do get involved in intimate relationships but have trouble staying the course or being really open and vulnerable within a close relationship. Defended distancers may be commitment phobic and very ambivalent about intimacy; they move in and out of relationships, often seeming to have one foot out the door when in an intimate relationship. Defended distancers may be a part of a couple but they remain emotionally and/or sexually walled off, so they are unavailable to meet their partner's relational needs.

This form of distancing can occur along a spectrum of behavior. Some defended distancers are actively resistant to emotional or sexual intimacy, refusing to share their feelings or erecting impenetrable sexual barriers, while others may not be aware that they are shut down. Some defended distancers use criticism and frequent conflicts to create distance even though they may be unaware that they are doing this.

At the far end of this spectrum is the unconscious process of *dissociation.* This form of distancing is so total that the person's body may be literally present but his or her mind and emotions have checked out.

The Commitment-Phobic Distancer

This style of distance regulation requires at least the start-up of potentially intimate relationships. In this style, the defended distancer finds a potential partner who will engage, at least for a while, in the Distancer Tango. (Note that the partner often appears to be a typical pursuer or a love addict but is actually another distancer in disguise.)

In this scenario, the distancer may first entice the potential partner, and then create an endless cycle of dramatic rejections, only to return once again to lure the same "victim" all over again. Often, this well-disguised style of commitment phobia produces a well-choreographed combination of distancing and pursuing. Couples can spend a lifetime doing the distancer-pursuer dance.

To get a deeper understanding of this style of distancing, let's watch a couple in action.

Jack and Diane's Story

Jack and Diane, the couple you read about earlier in this chapter, taught me to really respect the dizzying potency of the pursuer-distancer roller-coaster relationship. I also learned from them that what may look like a simple situation of one person as the distancer and the other as the pursuer can turn out to be two distancers in action.

At first, Jack appeared to be the pursuer. He and Diane found each other irresistible when they met one summer at the weekend wedding party of mutual friends. Jack's pursuit of Diane was very romantic; he felt a vibrancy that his life had been lacking for a while. They broke up and then made up many times before he was finally vanquished by Diane's stamina in their approach/avoidance marathon.

First Jack and Diane would declare their undying passion for each other in a manner worthy of an opera. Then Diane would abruptly change her mind and briefly banish Jack, only to beg him to return a little later. Jack was hooked. Although he vowed never to return each time Diane shoved him out the door, when she invited him to come back, he flew to her. Whenever he got angry and refused to forgive and forget, she ardently pursued him with gifts, notes, and, always, copious apologies for her previous rejection.

Diane's dramatic fluctuations exemplify one style of the defended distancer. What fueled Diane's role in this tango of approach and withdraw was Jack's stated desire for a deeper emotional and sexual closeness. Her fear of deeper intimacy and stronger commitment pushed Diane to dance backwards. As Jack pressed on with his desire by planning a future with Diane, the pace of their tango escalated. Diane was terrified by Jack's desire for closeness and commitment and, predictably, responded by ordering him away. Her explanations for her rejections changed each time.

During this courtship from hell, Jack wasn't conscious of his compliance in their relational dance. He saw himself as the victim, a helpless man with a doglike devotion to a capricious princess. He continued to offer himself to Diane, who, in turn, seemed determined to break his heart over and over again for the rest of his life.

Like many other couples who get stuck in the pursuit and distancing game, the person who is the "designated pursuer" usually has her or his own share of distancing tendencies. Jack, who turned out to be a closet distancer himself, was spared having to examine his own ambivalence because Diane so readily took full responsibility for the push-pull nature of their relationship. Nonetheless, Jack would have given up much sooner if he had not found something deeply satisfying in this operatic relationship.

Jack's Story

Jack returned to therapy with me years after I'd failed in my efforts to help him and Diane. Once again, he was in pursuit of an unavailable woman, and the parallels were so striking that he'd decided to return to individual counseling with me. He was now more willing to see that he too was a distancer when in a couple relationship.

He told me that he'd run into Diane not long before he recontacted me. Diane had apologized to him for the turmoil of their on-again off-again affair, and confided that she'd finally become aware that she had been severely traumatized from the impact of childhood sexual abuse. "So," Jack said to me, "I guess I finally have to stop blaming her and every other woman who's jerked me around, and figure out what's wrong with me."

Jack's style of distancing was to pursue women who were emotionally unavailable. To stay involved for as long as he had in these destructive relationships, he had had to maintain a very high level of denial. It had been very difficult for him to assert his right to receive better treatment because his self-esteem was so low.

The Ambivalence of the Defended Distancer

There are many variations in how the defended distancer operates. Although Diane typified the commitment-phobic defended distancer, other defended distancers, equally afraid of becoming emotionally or sexually vulnerable, act out more ambivalence in their attachments. While there are fewer makeup and breakup dramas, the distancer keeps holding back, never really capable of letting himself (or herself) get close to a partner.

The ambivalent distancer never seems to find the elusive perfect lover, yet he never gives up the quest. He may briefly partner with someone, then quickly move on to greener pastures. The ambivalent distancer can also stay within a relationship but strays repeatedly toward other objects of desire outside the committed relationship as a way of defending against a deeper connection with one person.

This form of distancing can be maddening for everyone involved. These distancers, just like the other types, are very vulnerable. They experience fear of closeness, chronic restlessness, and pervasive dissatisfaction. They usually feel frequent frustration, beaten down by lost opportunities, and an increasingly deep disappointment in themselves. They often long for the one who got away. Here's a typical illustration of this ambivalent distancing style:

Ben's Story

I glanced again at the page of new client information Ben had filled out in the waiting room. Ben was a self-employed carpenter and boat builder. He had been in psychotherapy before, although it appeared that he had never continued therapy for more than a few sessions. He was obviously anxious, his restless hands signaling his nervousness. He ran his fingers through his dark shaggy hair, buttoned and unbuttoned one shirt cuff, and periodically rubbed the arm of his chair. Then he settled in, crossing his arms across his chest, his hands locked under his armpits. His deep blue eyes held mine in a steady, challenging gaze.

"What brings you to see me?" I asked.

His steady gaze dropped. He rubbed his jaw, fashionably dark with just a shadow of stubble. He fiddled with his shoe, adjusted it, and peered at it as if he had just discovered his toes. Finally, he looked back at me, his eyes bright with tears. "It's what happens to me every time I get into a relationship," he said. "I can't seem to stay with anyone. Women end up hating me." He paused, then looked back down at his shoe. "I feel like a monster," he said, his deep voice so soft I could barely hear him.

"What kind of monster, Ben?" I asked.

He sighed, a big whoosh like a whale exhaling. "I don't really know. It always starts out fine, but then I realize it isn't right for me. I end up feeling bad about it, but I just have to leave once I realize that she's not the woman I've been looking for." He stopped and there was a long pause. Once again, his eyes met mine. He suddenly looked like a guilty little boy. "I feel like a monster," he continued, "because I hurt one woman after another. I know it isn't their fault. There's something wrong with me, but I don't know what to do."

Ben was a defended distancer whose ambivalence issues had created a smoke screen of perfectionism. Rather than understanding that he was a frightened distancer, he saw himself as a perfectionist; that is, he saw himself as someone whose need for perfection had made it impossible for him to find the partner he longed for.

While he told me about his series of failed relationships, he described himself as his own worst enemy. He wasn't happy as a single man, but at the age of forty-one he was about to give up. Ben was like many of the other men and women I'd met in my practice whose relationship histories were characterized by a deep ambivalence. Most of these people would have genuinely preferred being in lasting relationships, if only they had known how to achieve that state.

When the defended distancer is a perfectionist, he or she usually sets extreme standards for himself as well as for others. This type of distancer is tyrannized by self-doubt and a critical inner voice that never allows a partner to be "good enough." These types of distancers have a hard time making a firm decision to stay with anyone because they are driven by self-doubt and anxiety about making a mistake, or they become paralyzed with a strong rush of judgmental thinking.

Ben, like most distancers, was longing for the gifts that only intimate relationships can bring. He wanted a close relationship in which he could give and receive comfort.

During all of our subsequent therapy sessions, I learned that Ben repeatedly found himself in a cycle of initial delight about the new beloved, only to be followed by crushing disappointment. He never stayed single for long, craving the hopeful period of the courtship stage. As each promising new relationship deepened, Ben became skittish, and eventually he backed out under a cloud of apologetic guilt. Like other distancers, Ben was afraid of emotional commitment and the vulnerability that comes with that territory, but he dealt with his fear by turning it into an intensely critical inner voice that found fault with each new partner.

The Joker, Another Type of Defended Distancer

Another style of distancing is to use sarcasm and dark, bitter humor to defend against vulnerability in an intimate relationship.

Colin's Story

Colin was a middle-aged lawyer who drove women away because of his compulsive sarcasm and frequent bouts of anger, although one woman after another fell for his wit and compelling sexual energy. He crashed and burned through three marriages and many other relationships in between. Although each romance had its sparkling moments, inevitably, the women would leave him. Despite their early declarations of great love and affection, each one of Colin's ex-wives and girlfriends told him that they couldn't go on living in a state of defensive anxiety, forced to arm themselves against his constant irritability and harsh verbal attacks.

In the company of his fellow lawyers and grateful defendants, Colin was a different man, generous and fiercely protective in his defense of the vulnerable. Even though his anger and sarcasm would still surface, he never attacked his colleagues or clients in the same vicious way he went after his intimate partners.

Although Colin knew that he couldn't hold on to a relationship, for a long time he claimed not to care.

Distancing and Sexual Defensiveness

Both women and men also use various forms of sexual defensiveness to distance themselves from emotional intimacy. This can take the form of avoiding sexual interactions entirely, or shutting down while engaged in love-making.

Yvonne, the young woman you met very briefly at the beginning of this chapter, loves her boyfriend, but she can't stay present during sex. She shuts down her feelings, thoughts, and her physical responses, forcing herself to go through a sexual performance that she watches from a distance.

Danny, the young science-fiction writer, distances himself both sexually and emotionally from his girlfriend. He doesn't spend much time with her, and when they are together, he avoids feeling really close to her while they make love by fantasizing about being a sexual superhero. In this way, he can enjoy sex but he's completely detached from the physical reality of the two human beings who are actually connecting.

Exercise

Are You a Defended Distancer?

Use this scale to score your answers:

1 = This doesn't describe me at all.
2 = This describes my behavior a little bit.
3 = This describes my behavior in some ways.
4 = This describes quite a lot of my behavior.
5 = This is definitely me.

Rate yourself from 1 to 5 to answer the following statements:

1. When I start getting really involved with someone, I usually discover major flaws that I hadn't been aware of when we first got together. _____
2. When I start getting really involved with someone, I end up feeling seriously disappointed in who the person turns out to be. _____
3. Once I've been seeing someone for a while, I usually start feeling bored by that person or by the nature of that relationship. _____
4. In intimate relationships, I start to feel pressured to open up emotionally in ways that are uncomfortable for me. _____
5. In intimate relationships, I experience difficulties with my sexual vulnerabilities. _____
6. I go into my head a lot when emotional or sexual feelings start getting stirred up. _____
7. I have trouble making up my mind whether I want to break up or make up once a relationship really gets going. _____
8. I think intimate partners expect too much from me. _____
9. I feel increasingly suffocated as intimate relationships move beyond the initial courtship stage. _____

4 10. I keep my distance from partners by not seeing them too often, or not spending too much time alone with them. 2

Total score: 14

If your score was between 45 and 50, then you fit the profile of the defended distancer.

If you scored somewhere between 35 and 45, there are significant aspects of being very armored or defended that fit your relational style.

Now, just as you did in the last exercise, use the information you obtained from answering this questionnaire to make a few notes about yourself in your journal. Notice which aspects of being so defended seem to resonate most strongly with your experience of yourself. See if there are some aspects about yourself that you feel okay about and don't plan to change. Notice what upsets you the most. Which things would you most like to change?

The Distracted Distancer

The distracted distancer neglects the couple's need for closeness and intimacy, engaging full tilt in a wide variety of other activities. Distracted distancers put up an invisible smoke screen of activities between themselves and their partners, performing very subtle avoidance maneuvers in their preoccupation with children, work, family, friends, community service, faith-based activities, self-improvement… the list can go on and on. Distracted distancers can find time for everyone and everything, except for their partners. Note: In this distancing category, women are in the majority.

The "Superpartner" Distancer

Typically, distracted distancers are relationally missing even when they are publicly committed to their relationships. Instead of the tango dancing of defended distancers like Ben or Diane, or the firewalls put up by Colin, or the sexual distancing illustrated by Yvonne, the distracted distancer appears to be a dependable, thoughtful, and loving partner. This distancer wears the disguise of Superwoman or Superman, remembering to stop at the grocery store, taking the car in for regular tune-ups, and providing numerous important services that often benefit the partner.

So why does the partner complain? How much more wonderful could this superprovider be?

Sally's Story

Sally sees me periodically for "tune-up" sessions, even though these days, she is enjoying a closer relationship with her husband Howard. Sally used to employ the typical distracted distancer's style of using constant noncouple-centered activities to keep up her protective armor.

Sally was in her late forties when she first began working with me. She'd called me on the advice of a close friend who had suggested that if Sally didn't get some help, she was going to lose Howard. Sally's friend, a colleague of mine, thought I might be able to help.

When she first visited my office she said, "I'm so grateful that you could see me." She was beautifully dressed in flowing silks, scarves, and an accumulation of jewelry worthy of an African queen. She apologized for being late, and then for no apparent reason apologized for putting her coffee cup on the side table beside her. I would learn that Sally apologized more often than she did almost anything else.

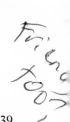

People always wanted more from her than she could give, she told me. "My friend Alicia, the woman who told me to call you, is like everyone else in my life. She gets really angry when I can't return her calls. I just get so overwhelmed and then I just have to

take a break. My friends all get mad at me once in awhile." She looked at me, smiled sheepishly, and said, "And then there's my husband… that's a really big problem."

Sally distanced herself emotionally in her efforts to restore her depleted energy. She retreated to someplace deep within herself. At times, she even distanced from her friends; not returning calls, ignoring e-mails, and failing to show up for appointments with her closest friends. The person she neglected most of all was Howard, although she couldn't admit this directly to him.

I reassured Sally that she was not alone, that other people also use indirect tactics to keep them from having to face problems in their relationships.

"I got married twice," Sally continued, "too young and gullible to know what I was getting myself into. I left my first husband when I realized I was being Mom; only I was his *mother. Then I tried again. I was looking for someone who was super-responsible. I married Howard because he was a nice guy and he seemed like he could come through. And, you know, he could." Sally laughed ruefully. She glanced at me before looking away again, something I would come to recognize as one way that she kept me at an emotional distance.*

"I'm not proud of this next part," she said, her tone painfully apologetic, "but I've never given Howard the love and affection he deserves. We got married when I was thirty. I was tired of taking care of my two kids and useless Husband Number One. So I just kind of ignored the fact that Howard might expect my love and care too. We were okay for a year or so, and then I panicked. He has chronic back trouble, and then he was told he had diabetes. I was so afraid I'd be stuck taking care of him."

Sally was the quintessential distracted distancer; she was unable to stop herself from pulling away when she felt overwhelmed by other people's needs; yet at the same time, she stayed very busy and productive so that she was well-defended from criticism. The distracted distancer may alternate between blaming herself about the way she shuts herself away from loved ones, and then complaining tearfully about how often she becomes overwhelmed by the demands of her partner, her friends, or her family. Instead of being able to set consistent limits, time and again the distracted distancer feels that she is under siege.

When this happened to Sally, sometimes she disappeared emotionally and even physically. Her appointments with me would be abruptly cancelled or missed, which gave me a taste of the impatience the others in her life must sometimes feel. Yet it was hard to be annoyed with her because she always seemed to be called away to help someone in need—one of her kids, a friend, a colleague at work.

Rick's Story

Rick is the poster boy for the distracted distancer, even though, at first glance, he would seem anything but distracted. (Rick is the superprotector father, husband, and worker you met earlier in the chapter.) Rick tried to take control of everything and everyone in his efforts to be a superprovider. After a while, this military style of marriage stopped working for his wife Carla, even though she had been grateful for many years for his strength, commitment, and devotion.

By controlling everything and everyone around him, Rick had closed himself off from being open to love. It took a while, but Carla finally realized that despite her husband's heartfelt efforts to be a good provider, she was lonely.

Distracted distancers may avoid intimacy by becoming workaholics, others by following creative pursuits, and still others by giving all they've got emotionally to their children while virtually ignoring the emotional needs of their partner. If we could watch these distancers in cartoon form, their time together as a couple would look like someone picking up a meal at the drive-up window of a fast-food restaurant.

Gender differences show up most prominently in this distancing style. Women are more likely to distance by being Supermom, while men typically distance themselves in their dedication to work or recreational pursuits. Women are also more likely to distance by becoming "crisis junkies": any crisis, whether their own or someone else's, will occupy them so that there is no time left for their partner. Both men and women may distance through excessive involvement in spiritual pursuits, just as both genders may neglect the couple relationship because they are so involved with an addiction. It could be an addiction to chemicals, food, gambling, online chat rooms, shopping, or even TV.

The distracted distancer is the most difficult to recognize, especially if the distancing activity is considered virtuous; that is, focusing on children, work, creative pursuits, or religious activities. Yet this distancer is in just as much trouble as the other two types. The distracted distancer may end up losing love completely. The once-patient partner eventually seeks divorce, an affair, or simply becomes relationally unavailable too, equally disengaged from the couple's well-being.

Exercise

Are You a Distracted Distancer?

Here is another diagnostic exercise to help you compare your behavior to this style of distancing. Use the same scale as in the previous exercises to score your answers:

1 = This doesn't describe me at all.
2 = This describes my behavior a little bit.
3 = This describes my behavior in some ways.
4 = This describes quite a lot of my behavior.
5 = This is definitely me.

1. I get so involved with my commitments (e.g., children, work, community activities). I really need my time, so there's little or no time for my partner. ______
2. I feel I don't get the appreciation I deserve from my partner for my commitments to ____________ (family, work, social causes, church, community service, etc.). ______
3. I don't stay involved with people who can't make room for my other commitments. ______

4. My passion for ______________ (creative pursuits, sports, working out, spiritual practice) doesn't allow much time for just hanging out with my partner. ~~3~~ 4
5. I believe that if my partner really valued what I spend my time doing, she (or he) wouldn't complain about our relationship. 3
6. I get restless or bored when I spend too much couple time with my partner. 1
7. I prefer groups more than one-on-one activities, e.g., I'd rather have dinner with a group of friends or family members than have a meal alone with my partner (or date). ~~1~~ 3
8. My partner needs too much of my time. Why can't he find someone else to talk to or walk with or just go see a movie by himself? ~~2~~ 4
9. I have trouble saying no when my partner wants time alone with me, so I just avoid letting it get to that point. ~~2~~ 4
10. I am so busy—I don't know why I still feel lonely. 5

Total score: 27

A score of 45 to 50 means you are probably more like the distracted distancers you just read about than you want to acknowledge.

If your score is between 35 and 45, do some thinking about what this means for you. Are you willing to consider that you may have to make some big changes in your time priorities if you want a more deeply connected partner relationship? What are you willing to consider changing? What do you feel okay about? What upsets you the most?

Couples Caught in the Distancer Trap

You may find it helpful to read about couples where both people distance in their own way. The following four couples each represent different challenges and issues:

Meet Luisa and Diego, a couple with a twist. They have reversed the traditional roles in which the man is viewed as the emotional distancer. Nevertheless, it doesn't seem to matter who is the emotional distancer; attempts at open communication do not go well for this couple.

Diego and Luisa's Story

Luisa and Diego married when they were young graduate students. Diego got his degree as a clinical social worker while Luisa was getting her MBA. They defy gender stereotypes, both in their careers (he's the one who takes care of people, while she manages numbers) and in how they express their emotions. Diego wants more emotional openness; he wants to share joys and sorrows, to cry companionably when they watch a sad movie.

Luisa is very uncomfortable with Diego's emotional openness and vulnerability. She grew up in a traditional family where the men were supposed to be strong and reassuring, to take care of their women, and to never show vulnerability. She sees Diego's openhearted style as a form of weakness. Luisa confided in couples counseling that Diego's preoccupation with emotional sharing is a sexual turnoff for her. He just doesn't seem manly enough.

When Diego had his turn, he told the therapist that Luisa disappoints him. He hinted that he is almost ready to go outside of the marriage to meet his emotional needs. He admitted that he has been spending a lot of time with a female colleague at work who is going through a divorce and who "understands the importance of emotional sharing."

This was a situation where the therapist was not alert to the deep issues of distancing. She followed the primary rule of couples counseling—more direct communication—and told Diego and Luisa to be more open and honest with each other during the therapy sessions. After several very painful meetings, Luisa walked out of the therapy. She accused Diego and the therapist of ganging up on her. "You want me to be just like the two of you," she said angrily, "just putting my private feelings out there for everyone to see. I'm not like that, and I can't change. And you're just a weakling, Diego."

Diego ended up having an affair with his coworker, and Luisa divorced him. This couple had a complicated history that could not be solved simply by trying to communicate better.

Exercise

Learning About Yourself Through Identification

You will be the expert here. Notice if you identify with any aspects of Luisa and Diego's situation. Write some notes, and if possible, talk this over with someone who feels safe to you. Here are the questions:

1. Do you see one person in the couple at fault here? No Both
2. Do you feel critical of Diego for allowing himself to get into an affair with his coworker? Yes
3. Do you see the root of the problem starting with Luisa because she refused to be more open emotionally? ____________
4. Do you identify more with Diego or Luisa? ____________
5. Have you ever been in a situation with someone who wanted you to be more open with your feelings than you wanted to be? Yes
6. If you believe that the therapist didn't adequately support Luisa, how could she have made it easier for the couple to communicate about their feelings? working to get each to adapt to the other's style

Reading Luisa and Diego's story may help to remind you that not everyone has the same beliefs about sharing emotions. It's interesting that even though Luisa and Diego share similar cultural roots, they have very different attitudes about emotional openness. Both Luisa and our next couple illustrate that, contrary to popular belief, women are not always comfortable talking about their feelings.

Chris and Beth are also a nontraditional couple. They, like Diego and Luisa, have communication issues. Their problem lies in their difficulties with conflict, which is another thorny issue for many distancers.

Chris and Beth's Story

The failure of indirect, strategic communication is not only a problem for heterosexual couples. Gay and lesbian partners are also troubled by such communication styles. Chris and Beth were trapped by their communication failures.

"Whenever I try to get Chris to talk about what's really going on for her," Beth told me, "she gives me the runaround. Her standard answer is 'I'm okay, but you obviously have something you need to talk about.' Or she says 'I don't want to talk about it right now,' but then she never does talk about whatever is bothering her."

Beth also complained that Chris distracts her from emotionally charged conversations by pointing out something they need to do around the house, or initiating a recreational activity or a shopping expedition. Chris makes sure that whatever they do puts the brakes on sharing anything that might be distressing. Their errands and home improvement marathons leave little time for intimate conversation.

"I don't see what the point is," Chris responds irritably. "Talking about everything usually just makes things worse. I don't want to end up fighting all the time the way my parents did. I'm perfectly content with our relationship just the way it is."

So, Beth gives up, immediately backing off. "I really do understand," she said. "Chris grew up in a violent home and it makes sense to me that she doesn't want to fight. Maybe we shouldn't be talking everything to death and making ourselves unhappy. What

I really want to talk about in our session today," she continued, deftly changing the subject, "is how soon we can both agree to retire so we can do all the things we want to do."

Chris and Beth are both participating in the slow death of the intimacy they share. Chris distances through verbal and nonverbal maneuvering. She is direct only about her commitment to their communication strategy of avoidance. She clearly states her fear: open, direct communication leads to fighting, and fighting is to be avoided at all costs. Beth colludes in the distancing dance by backing off and not asserting her own need to know and be known at a deeper level.

Exercise

Self-Assessment of Avoidance Patterns

Complete the following sentences to assess your tendency to choose avoidance rather than direct communication. You can use your answers to see how you are most likely to use avoidance as a distancing tactic.

1. When I know that someone doesn't agree with me, I usually place it in "agree to disagree"
2. If people close to me start to argue, I usually listen & respond / react
3. Getting along easily with others is important to me because I don't like fights
4. I often keep my opinions to myself rather than only w/ certain people
5. I often apologize for upsetting someone I care about because [illegible]
6. My parents argued 9/10 compared to other adults I grew up observing.
7. In my family, fighting was never much in the open

8. I generally don't get into conflict with others because I __________ __________ anger.
9. I avoid conflict because it __________ me.
10. In my ideal couple relationship, conflict is __________ __________ __________

Parenting and Distancing

Distancers can easily slip under the radar when the focus of the couple's unhappiness is on parenting issues. Here are a few examples of how couples can be so caught up in parenting issues that they may completely miss seeing the underlying distancing threats to their relationship as intimate partners.

Steven and Ruth, Superparents

Steven and Ruth are twenty-first-century parents who both play very active roles in their children's lives. They are a perfectly matched work team, showing up for every aspect of their children's lives. When they married and talked about raising children, they agreed that they would selflessly devote themselves to their children. Neither wanted to follow in the footsteps of their own parents who had been neglectful and abusive toward their children.

Although Ruth and Steven's dedication to their children is admirable, their life as a couple is barely alive. They are too tired to have time to have fun with each other and too vigilant about the children to relax and just enjoy making love. They collude in their distancing, and although neither one sees a problem in how they're living, the couple's intimacy is dying a slow death because they've been distancing for years.

This couple is very well-defended against any awareness that their life as a couple is dying on the vine. They are not experiencing the obvious erosion that occurs when one person wants intimacy while the other is totally absorbed in parenting. This is, unfortunately, both the good news and the bad news. Steven and Ruth may be lucky enough to get through the years of intense involvement with their children without losing their intimate connection with each other, but the danger is there. It would not be surprising if either person woke up one day and realized their marriage was over emotionally. Should this happen, either of these two could easily fall in love with someone new.

Sally and Howard

Sally and Howard are a good example of the couple that's in trouble even though Supermom is at the helm and they don't fight about parenting issues. As Sally's second husband, Howard was content to play whatever role Sally and the children wanted him to play: he would be the supportive stepdad or the more distant, hands-off husband with little involvement in the family's parent-child dynamics. He thought that the way Sally managed her job as mother was just fine, but he often felt that her preoccupation with the kids kept the two of them from having enough time with each other.

Sally used the kids to keep her distance from Howard. She was afraid to allow herself to depend on Howard and afraid to become more open in their couple intimacy. Her many hours at work were equaled by her hours as Supermom, and too often Howard was the last item on her list.

Ignoring the underlying distancing patterns that are at the heart of the couple's unhappiness is easy when the distancer is unaware that there's a problem. Simply urging Howard to become more involved in parenting would have been a mistake, one that is very commonly made by therapists, friends, and family. Sally needs help to see that (1) she is an active distancer, and (2) that Howard is capable of being much more involved in many parts of her life, including parenting.

If changes take place only in the domain of giving Howard more parenting opportunities, the underlying distancing will continue to undermine the couple's relationship.

Positive Aspects of Distancing

It is useful to distinguish among the basic categories and styles of distancing, but it is equally important to notice that there are many positive things that distancers have in common.

Distancers are motivated by an inherently logical quest for balance and self-protection. Their vacillations and avoidance patterns are often the best survival strategies he or she has been able to establish. Leaving the scene or using an approach/avoidance method has provided an escape route from feeling trapped by commitments, obligations, structures, or activities that may feel dangerous.

In some ways, distancers are ideally adapted to survive real danger because they are so quick to see the warning signs. The distancer has some very important survival skills, like always remaining alert, paying close attention to what's going on, being ready to move backwards or flee when danger may appear. Unfortunately, such accentuated vigilance can lead someone to mistake the smoke for the fire. Distancers may be unable to differentiate between real threats and benign people, places, and activities.

Respecting the Logic of Distancing

Within the distancer's cautious and vigilant pattern of holding back, there are seeds of reflection, discernment, and vision. These strengths may engender a deep spiritual practice nourished by the natural attraction to a peaceful, reflective life.

There is no doubt that distancers certainly can push their partners to the edge of screaming exasperation. Yet these people can also be valued friends, teachers, or advocates. Distancers can use their deep and thoughtful processes of discernment to become successful problem solvers because they avoid commitment to one idea or choice, and therefore can deliberate carefully and thoughtfully. Then, too, this style of response often provides the distancer with the ability to listen carefully to others. The distancer may be a treasured friend to a number of men and women who know they can count on her for carefully considered advice when they ask for it.

Finding Satisfaction in Time Alone

As we analyze the strengths inherent in these distancing patterns, it is notable that distancers have the capacity to assert limits and know the limits of their availability. Because of their potential for self-awareness, distancers are often able to find deep sources of self-generated solace.

Often, the capacity to spend time alone is an area of strength for distancers. Some people go to great lengths to avoid being alone. They may even believe there's something wrong with them if they are alone for any significant amount of time. In contrast, the distancer who deeply appreciates time alone can be very resilient in adapting to a variety of situations. There are times when one has to be alone. Being comfortable with being alone means the person is able to work alone for long periods of time, or to accomplish basic life tasks alone, or to engage in recreational activities alone. The distancer is often well-suited for bigger challenges, too, like living alone, being alone when ill or injured, traveling alone, and surviving the loneliness of grief.

Although someone may be self-sabotaging by disappearing or distancing behaviors, the powerful forces that drive that person to seek solitude can also be beneficial to creativity. The creative person, that is, the artist, musician, writer, woodworker, photographer, decorator, researcher, inventor, landscaper, gardener, builder—any creative person—thrives when able to spend enough time alone to engage in uninterrupted creative pursuits.

Creating distance can also be useful and necessary. Someone like Sally might need time alone because she has spent too many years being deluged with other people's needs, activities, conversations, noise, and demands. Sally grew up in a big family and had little time for herself and her own needs. Some of her need for time alone is a healthy choice to make up for her years of meeting others' needs, giving herself the gift of solitude. There are work situations that may require someone to spend the majority of her time alone. If you spend hours underneath the hood of a car, on a tractor, writing poems, fixing computers, or making jewelry, you undoubtedly need a lot of solitary time.

Choosing Other Priorities

Note that relational distancing may be a conscious choice to prioritize something else. It is possible when all is said and done, that at this time in your life you may not want to be in an intimate relationship. Both men and women may choose very demanding career paths that don't allow them the necessary time to develop and nurture an intimate relationship. When there are children, because women are still most commonly the primary caregivers, women, especially, may feel they must choose between committed motherhood or a deeply engaging relationship. Giving up the time it takes to engage in intimate relationships may also feel necessary to someone with an all-consuming creative or spiritual calling.

You're on Your Way

You're now fully engaged in the process of challenging your inner distancer simply by allowing yourself to think about the stories and new ideas you've just read. Learning which style of distancing best describes your distancing behavior will help you to begin the work of leaving loneliness behind. All it takes is a little curiosity and willingness to be open to a new way of understanding yourself.

In the following chapters, we will follow the journeys of the people you have just been introduced to, showing how they have been able to find greater happiness in their close relationships. Learning what they had in common with many others and analyzing their individual patterns of distancing was the beginning for each of them. They also jump-started their recovery by learning to identify and embrace both the strengths and the logic contained within their styles of distancing.

By getting to know other distancers, you have begun your work in identifying and accepting yourself. As you think about the hallmark characteristics of distancing, and as you discover that your story matches one or more of the people in this chapter, you are becoming more informed about the specific ways you engage in distancing. You have begun to identify with the potential strengths as well as the self-harming patterns of the distancer. As you try on each of these styles for "fit," you may decide that one of these descriptions is your dominant style overall. Or you may recognize that it describes you in some aspects of your life, but does not apply in other areas.

Once you begin to identify your patterns of distancing, you can take the necessary steps to analyze why you have been regulating emotional distance in the ways that you do. Then you can begin the work of trying something new.

It is important to honor the strengths contained within each of these styles. Whatever your methods of distancing may be, until now this has been the best way you've found to survive. You are fully capable of change, but you can also hang onto your old survival skills as long as you need to. This isn't a race and there are no deadlines.

2 Step One: Raising Your Awareness

Before you start working on Step One, which is expanding your awareness, let's take a look at the ways you may have approached intimacy challenges in the past.

Red Herrings and Incomplete Solutions

There are a myriad of reasons why each of us takes the time we do to finally change our unhappiness in our relationships. It doesn't matter if you're sixteen or sixty—you can change your patterns if you want to. But to help you find a more self-compassionate way to examine your past patterns, let's first take a look at some of the reasons why it's taken this long. Some of your past obstacles to change may lie within your own personality, while others may have come from bad advice and incomplete solutions to solving the dilemma of intimacy.

Floating Down the River of Denial

It is quite common for the distancer to lack self-awareness when it comes to assessing what's going wrong in the relationship domain. Many people go through life without consciously understanding what makes their relationship patterns troubling or simply dull and lackluster. Few men and even fewer women would describe themselves as distancers. Yet even though we may not have the words to name ourselves, every distancer knows the experience of chronic loneliness. Distancers share the general feeling of being incomplete, of not feeling fully connected to others.

Isolation or loneliness, especially within a couple relationship, often goes unspoken and unnamed, flying below the radar of self-awareness for both men and women. Distancers can find this kind of denial very comforting. It's easy to think, "Oh, it's not so bad. I can go on like this. It's not going to kill me." Denial is a very effective tool of self-protection for people who were violated, shamed, and threatened when they were children. Distancers are scared of being vulnerable in relationships, so denial becomes a very attractive option.

Learned Helplessness

Even when distancers reach the point of being seriously miserable, we often believe there's nothing that we can do about it. I used to believe that I was doing the best I could. I thought that my failure to find the "walking into the sunset" ideal relationship was caused by circumstances beyond my control. Sometimes I blamed my partners. Other times, I thought that my traumatic childhood experiences had doomed me to failure, even though I continued jumping into relationships with a kind of mindless optimism. Quite often, the people I chose were distancers themselves.

I have since learned both in my personal experiences and my work as a therapist that many distancers attribute their relationship dissatisfaction to external events: losing a job; moving to a new city; raising teenagers; dealing with chronic pain; or lacking access to desirable partners. You may have thought it's your partner's fault (past or present), or it's because you just haven't met the right person, or it's the fault of your in-laws or the family you grew up in. Even those of us who view love as a "no-fault" venture, i.e., no one is to blame when a relationship fails, may doubt there's anything we haven't already tried that would make our relationships more satisfying.

The Fear Factor

Distancers may resist change by convincing themselves they are simply doomed never to experience the fairy-tale rapture of "true love," or even if they should experience it, they fear that love might vanish instantly like a dream. In addition to not having enough information about the dynamics of distancing, many people resist change because they are afraid of getting hurt or even of being permanently wounded. We grow up expecting to be blinded by "true love," even when it turns out to be all smoke and mirrors. From fairy tales, popular songs, movies, and advertisements we learn that although love is exciting and glamorous, it often ends up breaking your heart.

If love hurts so much, many distancers ask themselves why risk exposing their deep relational vulnerability underneath the mask?

Glimmering pictures of blissful love are too often followed by bitter disillusionment and heartache. Couples expert Terrence Real, in his book *How Can I Get Through to You?* (2002, p. 33), reminds us that "one of the few stable statistics in our fast-changing world is our rate of divorce, which has hovered between 40 and 50 percent for the last thirty years." Why would you believe that you could make a lifelong relationship work, knowing that 40 to 50 percent of all couples are as likely to break apart as to stay together? Why not go with the flow and settle for whatever you've got right now?

Missing the Boat: Myths and Mistakes

Oversimplifying love's complexity accounts for many failed attempts to find and keep true intimacy. Many of the obstacles to happiness in love relationships arise from distracting or incomplete solutions. Of course, there is no one solution to the complex dilemmas of failed love, but narrow, oversimplified views of the problem are routinely proposed by professionals, talk-show hosts, and well-meaning friends and family members. Nonetheless, understanding some of the common pitfalls that have tripped up many who sought help with their problems about love may help you to stop blaming yourself.

Since people first began pursuing and rejecting their mates, other people have probably been giving them advice about love. In our time, the love experts have generated a steady stream of books, articles, and talk shows about improving the experience of love. Movies, TV shows, songs, poems, and novels provide us with an ever-changing menu of love's joys and heartbreaks. Yet with all this attention that we humans give to love, penguins, whales, and numerous other life-forms seem to be much more successful at it than we are. Why do we have such a hard time making love work for us?

One answer to that question is there are a cluster of myths and a number of incomplete solutions that may be involved in continuing to keep us from getting the love we want and deserve.

Open Communication: The Magic Bullet

Undoubtedly, the most common advice about creating good relationships is to improve communication. There are countless variations on this theme. You, too, have probably been told that better communication will magically create the walk into the sunset where you will live happily ever after with your beloved.

The unhappy husband grumbles, "Why can't she just tell me what she wants from me? Am I supposed to read her mind? She says we don't communicate. What's that supposed to mean?"

His wife sighs. She wants him to want to talk to her about the things that upset him. She also wants him to understand her, to know what's going on with her emotionally, without her having to explain. It seems so simple to her and so baffling to him.

The couples therapist tells them to choose fifteen minutes from each day when they won't be interrupted by children or work. They are supposed to talk to each other about their feelings, to lovingly listen to each other, and to find ways to communicate their support for each other. When they come back to the next session, it's no surprise they are more upset than ever about their relationship because they couldn't do the assignment.

Opening up communication is rarely as easy to do as it sounds, especially for the distancer. Unguarded, direct communication is a complicated challenge for men and women who are classic distancers. Although the couple you just met represent gender stereotypes, for the emotionally guarded man and the woman who yearns to be better emotionally "read" by her husband, direct communication can be a challenge for both of them. This impasse in communication can't be "fixed" just by a simple directive to let down their guard and be more open with each other.

My experience as a therapist and as a recovering distancer has taught me that it's easier said than done for distancers to open up communication with their partners. Distancers have deep-seated reasons for avoiding the vulnerability of open direct communication. If they could simply switch to a more open communication style, they would.

Strategic Communication: The Retro Solution

Sometimes, couples are advised to try indirect, strategic communication. Strategic communication allows the couple to avoid being direct and honest about anything that potentially could open up uncomfortable feelings or conflict. Couples who try to protect their intimacy engage in a sort of chess game that maneuvers the conversations around important issues and feelings rather than discussing those issues. However, believing that the relationship will survive by using indirect, manipulative communication or by avoiding problematic issues can be as unhealthy and shortsighted as the "open honest communication" method.

One familiar example of strategic communication is the age-old advice given to women about how to land and keep their man. "Let him think he's smarter than you, stroke his ego, don't let him know that you can beat him in tennis..." The parallel version of strategic communication takes place when men pretend to agree with their female partners to "humor" them. "I'm sure you're right, dear," says the husband vacantly as he ignores his wife's impassioned distress about her brother's iron-fisted control of the upcoming family holiday.

Gender Myths: Me Tarzan, You Jane

Another cause for couple trouble is the assumption that men are distancing when they express their emotions through action rather than by talking. Another aspect of this oversimplified view is the assumption that because women are more likely to talk about their feelings, they are never the distancers in relationships.

As you begin to learn more about the ways that women do, in fact, distance, you may be surprised. The stereotypical man might be able to hide his emotions under the brim of his John Deere cap, but his wife may be distancing by using sex as a bargaining tool, or being disconnected from her body while making love. Women can also distance by giving their quality time and attention only to their kids, friends, and family; in short, by focusing on everyone but their partner.

Experts often unwittingly collude in maintaining the loneliness of the couple by attributing all major relationship problems to gender differences. Couples become convinced they are doomed to loneliness in their intimate relationships, constricted by the narrow definitions of traditional gender stereotypes. From Tarzan and Jane to King Kong grasping the tiny female in his great fist, we continue to be sold the stereotypes of males and females as radically different species. This relegates the one-dimensional man to be the John Wayne strong silent type, and the woman to be his fragile, emotionally volatile "better half." How could two such constricted human beings connect deeply either emotionally or sexually?

Men were still viewed as the distancers in intimate relationships by the women's liberation generation in the 1970s and '80s. They were often portrayed as hopelessly defective in the relationship department. Although the '70s produced a counterbalancing image of more competent women, the male stereotype merely shifted slightly, morphing into Robert Bly's Iron John (1990). This version of maleness promoted an image of macho virility that perpetuated the myth of male incapacity for deep emotional intimacy with women and children.

Then, we read that men and women evolved on different planets (Gray 1992). Yet again, gender differences were accentuated. The people from Venus (women) are assumed to be love addicts while the other species from Mars (men) continue to live in their caves and avoid intimate communication.

Overstating gender differences lets women off the hook when it comes to owning their identity as distancers. The assumption that men and women are so totally different from each other also underestimates men. Many men long for love and intimacy in couple relationships. If all those men from Mars just wanted to get laid, there would be easier ways to go about it than committing to a long-term, live-in relationship that usually requires monogamy, child-rearing, and a promise to remain loving through sickness and health.

Men should not be shamed into believing that they are less fluent in the language of emotions and desires than women. Men may demonstrate their love by actions rather than through verbal expression, but they are also too easily discouraged from talking about matters of the heart. And women are too often led to believe that because they are more accustomed to talking about their feelings, they are off the hook in the distancing department.

The Problem Is Sex

Focusing too narrowly on sexual satisfaction is another mistake that can interfere with genuine intimacy. Both men and women can experience satisfying sex but still be lonely distancers. Conversely, some people can achieve deep levels of intimacy even when the relationship is no longer sexual.

It's easy to become confused about the difference between sex and intimacy because the word "intimacy" is frequently used as a euphemism for sex. Many layers of distancing behavior can be buried under the belief that the problem with intimacy is all about sex. "She won't open up with me" is the frequent complaint of the male partner who feels shut out sexually but doesn't fully comprehend the underlying complexity of the problem.

Through the gradual process of breaking down old taboos, beginning with the sexual liberation movement of the '60s, there has been increasing cultural permission for both men and women to be open about what they want sexually. In contrast with the sexual repression of previous decades, this is a good thing. But even sexual freedom can end up being a problem if it is the sole focus of change.

Attributing all relational problems to past traumatic experience also can be just as problematic as thinking that relationships will be automatically transformed by simply learning better sexual skills. Whether or not an individual has experienced sexual distress in the past, it is a mistake to believe that getting good sex therapy will be the panacea. This can be particularly disastrous if sex therapy becomes a series of anatomy lessons for the purpose of reaching an advanced level of sexual gymnastic ability.

Good chemistry and good sexual skills may help a relationship to work, but focusing all the solutions in the sexual arena can leave the heart of the relationship to somehow fix itself. This is similar to other oversimplified solutions to love's challenges, like believing that better communication will be the magic bullet, or that you have to live with loneliness because you've fallen for the modern myth that you and your partner are from different planets.

When Parenting Interferes with Intimacy

Parenting is a very demanding and very important part of adult life for many women and men, but, unfortunately, it can seriously erode couple intimacy. When professionals or friends collude in keeping the focus entirely on parenting issues, the underlying distancing in the couple's behavior can escape detection and leave one or both partners trapped in continuing loneliness.

This form of distancing happens most often when one parent is much more involved with the children than the other. Another variation in eroded intimacy occurs when one parent becomes jealous of the other's closeness with the children, which sometimes leads both parents to become distancers. Another type of erosion in the couple relationship can take place when both parents are so consumed with parenting their children that they have no time left over to nurture themselves as a couple. Still another scenario happens when the parents engage in major battles around child-rearing issues, and by so doing demolish their capacity to feel tenderness and affection for each other.

All of these dilemmas require intervention, but focusing exclusively on the parenting issues may overlook yet another kind of distress. In many of these situations, parents may use the need to nurture their children to distance from true intimacy with each other, without having any idea they are doing so.

When the Past Threatens Love

Too much or too little focus on the past can also lead to intimacy failures. Sometimes, the past can obstruct necessary repairs to current intimacy when there is denial of its impact. On the other hand, experiences from the past can remain so central to someone's emotional life that the current relationship (or potential partner) becomes eclipsed.

Some people distance from intimacy because they haven't been willing to look at their past relationships. They haven't come to terms with either the pain of the past or its lessons. Other people distance from relationships in the present by focusing too much of their attention and energy on their past.

"If Only She Didn't..."

Another major mistake is to focus too completely on one person's problems or impairments. This happens when one person is consumed with an addiction to a chemical substance or to work or gambling or online chat rooms, or any other addictive preoccupation. "Everything will be okay for us when he stops drinking (or overworking or... fill in the blank)" is a common myth verbalized by vast numbers of people who believe that the relationship can be saved by a change in one partner.

This also happens when one person is struggling with emotional problems like depression, anxiety, bipolar disorder, or attention-deficit disorder. The partner, friend, or therapist lowers the other partner's expectations for intimacy by saying things like, "She can't help it… she's depressed."

Currently, perhaps the most common reason for intimacy to suffer or vanish entirely is an exclusive focus on someone's history of past trauma and the resulting issues. Talk shows, professional helpers, friends, and family members perpetuate the myth that the trauma must be resolved before the relationship problems can be addressed.

After many years of working with adults who have experienced past traumas, I've learned that it is never really possible to wrap up the trauma work and then move on to dealing with relationships. It is more productive to determine how everything is related and then to address all aspects of the trauma's legacy, including its effect on creating healthy intimacy.

Learning to Increase Your Awareness

In this chapter, you will be working on Step One: Raising your awareness. Awareness is the first tool you need to open your heart and tame the runaway distancer part of yourself. Think of awareness as a very active process of change rather than just a reminder to pay attention. Simply becoming aware—fully conscious—can radically change your capacity to give and receive love. Awareness, at the deepest level, means a willingness to change your whole life.

This may sound abstract or even unbelievable unless you have grown up in a culture where the practice of awareness is at the root of a spiritual practice, or you have incorporated awareness practice as a daily part of your life. As you will learn by doing Step One, cultivating awareness is anything but abstract. It is a very real, one-day-at-a-time process of learning to focus in new and deeper ways.

Learning to cultivate and raise your awareness is a lifelong process. Awareness is a multipurpose tool to help you with the most important learning experience of your life: how to leave loneliness behind and discover lasting love.

Active Awareness: Turning Arrows into Flowers

Buddhist teacher and writer Pema Chödrön tells this story about the power of awareness in *Comfortable with Uncertainty* (2002, p. 40): "On the night the Buddha was to attain enlightenment, he sat under a tree. While he was sitting there, the forces of Mara (the Buddhist equivalent of evil or obstacles) shot arrows at him to distract him from becoming enlightened, but with awareness he turned their weapons into flowers."

You will be learning awareness skills that have the power to turn your own inner torments into flowers. Each of the areas in which you develop your awareness skills will lead you to the place where you will feel safe and empowered and ready for the work of remembering (Step Two) and the challenges of making new connections (Step Three). You will learn to cultivate the flowers of new awareness in the following areas:

- Awareness of your own natural learning style and process
- Awareness of how your mind and body are connected
- Awareness of your self-image, the story you tell yourself and others about who you are
- Awareness of the tactics you use to hang on to your distancing style, i.e., externalizing blame (it's her fault, not mine), experiential avoidance (avoiding feelings, interactions, risk-taking), denial, dissociation, addiction, learned helplessness
- Awareness of how you are influenced by your connections to others, how social and cultural contexts affect you, how you feel and act in couple relationships
- Awareness of the fears, anxieties, and losses that you've been trying unsuccessfully to bury

Acceptance

As you learn to cultivate awareness, you will be engaged in an active process of acceptance. This means that you will be absorbing and assimilating new information. You will continue the work you've already begun in the preceding chapter, that of identifying your style or profile as a distancer. Acceptance means testing out your acceptance of your inner distancer, allowing yourself to sit with it, let it in, keep it in focus, and not run away from your awareness.

To help you stay focused, you will continue using the exercises in the book, writing in the journal that will become the new story of who you are, and learning at many levels how to accept your new experiences of heightened and expanded awareness.

Willingness

Willingness is an essential component of awareness. Making an active commitment to willingness means that you keep yourself open to new ideas, new insights, and new possibilities; it means that you are willing to learn new things about yourself and your relationships. You will practice the willingness to become fully conscious, to accept what you are learning about yourself, and to try out your new awareness-based skills.

Building Your Awareness Skills

There are four categories of awareness skills that you will be using in the Awareness, Remembering, and Connecting (ARC) model. These skills provide tools to help you become more fully and richly present in every aspect of your life. Here are the four skills that will be transformative, no matter how you choose to use them in your life:

1. You will learn to practice mindfulness, which is the practice of being more fully present or conscious.

2. You will deepen your general awareness of how you perceive your world: that is, how you think, how you feel, and how you act.

3. You will develop a curious, open mind in observing how other people feel, think, and act in relationships.

4. You will develop a general relational awareness of yourself as you relate to people who do not fall into the category of "intimate" or "couple" or "potential partner."

Cultivating Mindfulness

Over the past several decades, the Western world has slowly begun to adopt some traditional Eastern practices. Learning to meditate, doing yoga, and practicing mindfulness have transformed the lives of many people who were living fast-paced, goal-centered lives. We see evidence of these Eastern influences in how many people in the United States have learned to meditate and practice deep breathing to calm and center themselves. "Practicing mindfulness" may be a very familiar idea to you, or you may be considering it for the first time. In either case, it is an essential part of the ARC model, at the bedrock level of transforming your relationships. Remember, "ARC" stands for awareness, remembering, and connecting.

Defining Mindfulness

It is way beyond the scope of this book to provide comprehensive instruction on what mindfulness is all about. People devote themselves to the study of mindfulness in workshops and other groups, and spend years learning to incorporate mindfulness in their lives. In the work we are doing together, we'll define mindfulness by describing how it works.

Mindfulness entails slowing down and really paying attention to what's going on inside you. It means that you pay attention to the root of being alive: your breathing. Mindfulness requires you to notice how your body is feeling and what is happening with the thoughts that circle around in your mind. Practicing mindfulness directs you to focus on bringing yourself into a state of being centered, calm, and alert. Mindfulness means being fully conscious so that at all levels of your being, you are fully awake.

Exercise
Mindful Breathing

Whether you've never practiced mindful breathing before or you've been doing mindfulness practice for years, spend a few minutes with this basic exercise. Take a little time right now to focus on your breathing. Try to make sure that you won't be interrupted for at least five minutes or so. Choose the quietest place available. Get yourself into a comfortable seated position so that you can focus on your breathing.

You may or may not want to close your eyes to do this breathing exercise. The risks of closing your eyes range from falling asleep to feeling unsafe or dissociating in some way that keeps you from staying present for this important learning experience. If you prefer to do it with your eyes open, just look down at the floor, not focusing on what you're seeing, and think about looking inside rather than outside yourself. This will help you to stay present.

- Now, gradually slow down your breathing by pausing briefly at the end of your out breath (the exhale) and then again at the end of your in breath (the inhale).

- Check your muscles to see if they are relaxed, paying special attention to relaxing the muscles in your hands, your shoulders, and your belly.

- Focus your attention on the experience of breathing, just noticing the feeling of breathing in, pausing, breathing out, pausing, and so on. See if you can keep your attention on just your breath for a few minutes. (If you haven't done this kind of focused breathing before, don't expect yourself to be able to do more than five minutes at first.)

- After a little while of slowing down your breathing and keeping your focus on your breath for a few minutes, notice again if your muscles have stayed relaxed.

- Finish this exercise by opening your eyes or bringing your attention back to your surroundings. How did doing this make you feel? Were you able to stay focused on your breath most of the time, or did you notice your mind jumping from thought to thought, or were you distracted by external noises, or tension, or pain in your body?

Don't worry if it was difficult to do this mindfulness practice for the first time. Everyone has trouble at first. It isn't a normal activity for most of us living in a busy, loud, goal-driven world to do this kind of breathing awareness exercise.

How Mindfulness Practice Will Help Your Relationships

As you gradually learn to be more fully conscious in many aspects of your life—your breathing, your thoughts, your body—you will become increasingly good at noticing what's going on when you are engaged in interactions with others. You will be able to observe yourself, noticing what kind of distancing messages your mind may be giving you, or noticing how the other person responds to what you are doing or saying. By increasing your overall level of awareness through mindfulness practice, you will begin to feel much more capable of thinking and acting in new ways in difficult areas of your life, especially in your intimate relationships.

The following story will illustrate for you how this can work.

Yvonne's Story

Yvonne had spent too long dreading the weekends. On weekdays, she was quite content with her life and her relationships. She went to work, had occasional dinners out with friends, went to her weekly chorus rehearsal, and worked out at the fitness club on the way home from work three times a week. She also enjoyed her nightly phone conversation with her boyfriend Mike, who lived two hours away in Boston.

Mike and Yvonne spent almost every weekend together. They loved going for drives in the country, hiking, and movies. They cooked together, played with Yvonne's cats, and spent hours talking about everything that mattered to each of them, except sex.

Yvonne was tortured by her discomfort with sex. She was a defended distancer whose primary problem was feeling sexually shut down. Although Mike and Yvonne made love at least once every weekend, Yvonne had a very hard time staying present during their love-making. Her body would remain actively engaged in the love-making, but she wasn't really there. She felt numb physically, her mind went off to more comfortable places, and her emotions would get so bottled up that at the end of the sexual interlude she would become irritable and depressed.

Yvonne had worked on this problem in psychotherapy. She knew that the roots of her distress were related to having been sexually abused by her older brother, and she was able to talk about her sexual distancing in the privacy of the therapist's office. She kept Mike in the dark, both literally and figuratively. She was afraid to tell him how shut down she was, even though she knew that he knew.

For Yvonne, using mindfulness practice was the key to a big turnaround for her relationship with Mike. She and Mike began to sit together to do some meditating. They both learned how to engage in mindful awareness.

One Saturday, Mike suggested that they do their practice of mindful breathing and meditation right before they made love.

To Yvonne's delight, moving from a place of mindfulness with Mike into love-making with him allowed her to stay more present. Once she was able to stay in her mind and body—a little bit at a time—she became able to allow herself to play a more active part in guiding Mike to give her sexual pleasure. It was a huge breakthrough for her when she became capable of staying aware of who it was she was in bed with, that in the present moment she was making love with her gentle, kind boyfriend and not being molested by a violent ghost from her traumatic past.

Although mindfulness practice does not magically transform all the places where distancers may feel helpless or hopeless, it is a tool that can gradually open many doors. You can begin incorporating mindfulness in many or all parts of your life. Try doing the mindful breathing practice once a day for five minutes.

Daily practice will help you to use mindful breathing spontaneously at other times when you need to calm and center yourself.

Deepening and Expanding Your Self-Awareness

We are all experts on ourselves. We know how we perceive the world, how we respond emotionally, how we generally relate to others. Often, however, we don't know we are experts; we don't know what we know. Who we are biologically influences the areas about which we are more aware. So does our accumulated life experience. Because I'm an expert on myself, I'll use myself as an example of how one person perceives and responds to the world.

I have always had very high energy, physically. I have rapid responses to all forms of stimulation through all of my senses, and my energy level ranges from active to hyper, even with the natural brakes of getting older. My rapid response system means that I feel physical pain and physical pleasure very quickly and very intensely. It also means that I have trouble staying still. I have a generally heightened awareness of sounds, smells, tactile sensations, my visual surroundings, and even taste.

The good news about my heightened levels of awareness is that I easily take in so much of whatever is pleasurable. The bad news is that I'm uncomfortably sensitive to negative experiences. At the biological level, for instance, I have a low pain threshold, and a strong negative response to loud noises, bad smells, or unpleasant tastes.

Because I am constantly taking in so much of what's happening around me, I'm better prepared to see and react to danger than many other people. On the other hand, it's sometimes energetically draining to be so hypervigilant; there are too many ordinary situations where my immediate impulse is to rescue, protect, freeze, or flee.

I've also been shaped by my personal experiences and the social messages and practices surrounding me. My experience as a child who felt loved influenced who I am in all kinds of relationships. But I was also shaped by my experience as a child who was forced to be my mother's emotional caretaker and my father's sexual plaything and punching bag.

These personal childhood experiences were mediated by adult relationships and the culture I grew up in and live in today. This means that I'm influenced by being a woman, a person who came of age during the civil rights movement, and someone who's spent most of her life in one geographical place—the town where I grew up and still live.

Everything I've just described played a role in my awareness of how I perceive and respond to the world. Everything I am aware of about who I am helps me to understand why I respond to closeness and intimacy in the way that I do. Self-awareness at all these levels also helps me to know the best ways for me to learn and to make big changes in my life.

The following exercise will guide you to expand your awareness of how you perceive, think, and act.

Exercise

The Self-Awareness Scan

Think over the week that just passed. Choose one particular incident or episode from your week, an event that was particularly memorable. It could be something that stands out because it was unusually pleasant, or unusually sad, or because it really got to you in some way—it stirred up negative feelings or made you really stop and rethink something.

Try to keep the parameters of the episode relatively simple. For example, you might decide to choose something that took place in a short span of time, like one conversation at work, or a part of a walk. When you have this incident in your mind, write a one-paragraph description, a very short summary of what happened. Keep it simple. When you've written this brief description, take some time to relive the incident or event in your mind, going over as much detail as you wish. When you are finished, look at the following categories and use them to figure out what is the clearest part of your memory of the whole experience:

- Feelings you had (your emotional responses)
- Your senses in remembering the details (sounds, smells, visual impressions, the feel of anything your body had contact with, the taste of anything you might have eaten or had to drink during the incident)
- Your thoughts in response to the episode, for example, "This is really unfair," or "This will have a big impact on..." or "How does this compare to something that happened before? How does this contrast with other experiences I've had?"
- How your body felt
- What your body did, that is, it got very jumpy, started sweating, went numb
- What other people were doing or saying
- What you believe others were feeling or thinking
- Fantasies you may have had about being somewhere else or doing something else
- Others you wished were present for you
- Others you wanted to protect or share this experience with
- Anything you did during or after the episode that relates to your spiritual practice

You may want to try doing several different exercises like this. Include good experiences as well as disturbing ones. After doing this a few times, you will begin to notice some dominant patterns in how your awareness works.

Remember: There is no right or wrong (or better or worse) way to perceive the world. The important thing is to develop your awareness in the ways that work best for you so that you can use these skills to grow and to find better solutions to the challenges you face.

Cultivating Curiosity

Most teachers, writers, and others who work with awareness skills do not include curiosity. However, my observations over many years have taught me to value curiosity as an extremely important part of cultivating awareness. This becomes obvious when you think about how children learn.

A small child's curiosity is at the core of what motivates many important learning experiences. A child learns most of the most critical survival skills by being curious, which leads to learning about boundaries and limits. The child learns about many things: how something works, what a cat or a dog is likely to do, what objects taste, feel, smell, and sound like—all because of the innate sense of curiosity that leads to exploration.

Curiosity is a vital part of any important relationship. The more you can cultivate your curiosity about the other people in your life, the more you will move toward them. Curiosity will also lead you to feel more secure with the people you are close to because you'll have a pretty good sense of what they're likely to think, feel, say, or do.

You've probably been appreciative of the people in your life who've been curious about who you are. That's because it feels good to have someone ask you how you are doing, and know that he or she is asking a real question; that the person is curious enough and cares enough about you to want a real answer.

Now, here's a self-diagnosis exercise you can do to check out how active your sense of curiosity is.

Exercise

Rating Your Sense of Curiosity

Use the scale of 1 to 5, with 5 being "this is very true for me," 4 meaning "this is mostly true for me," 3 being "this is true for me about half of the time," 2 meaning "this is true for me occasionally," and 1 being "this is rarely true for me."

1. I ask my friends lots of "what's going on with you" questions. 2
2. I ask my kids (if relevant) lots of "what's going on with you" questions. 1
3. I ask my partner (if relevant) lots of "what's going on with you" questions. 4
4. I want to know how the other people at work are doing and I ask them a lot of questions. 1
5. I ask a lot of questions when I'm getting to know someone new. 3
6. In most situations, I wonder what the other people who are involved are thinking. 2
7. In most situations, I wonder what the other people who are involved are feeling. 4
8. I often wonder what the other people in my family are feeling about certain things. 2
9. I would like to know much more about what my partner is thinking or feeling, even if I don't usually ask. 4
10. I often wonder what my life would be like if I were the citizen of another country or from a different ethnic or racial background. 1

Total score: 26

If you rated yourself 5 on most of these questions, then you have a very healthy sense of curiosity. Good for you! You can move right on to the next section of this chapter.

If you scored lower on questions 1 to 5 than you did on questions 6 to 10, then you may be very curious, but are hesitant to ask others directly about themselves. This could be because of family or cultural values that you've learned about not being too direct, not "prying," or "staying out of other people's business." Give yourself permission to allow your curiosity to be more assertive. See what happens when you ask people the questions that you have wondered about but have been keeping to yourself. You may be surprised at how many people actually like being asked about themselves, especially what they think and feel about people, places, and events.

If you averaged 3 or lower on the answers to all ten questions, then you need to find out what holds you back from asking questions or being more curious about other people. In your journal, keep track of any ideas you come up with about why you are not especially curious about others. Are you too anxious or nervous or fearful to think about what's going on with other people? Are you too busy just trying to get through all the tasks right in front of you to be curious? Are you so worried about what others are thinking about you that it doesn't leave any room to be curious about them?

Julie

Remember Julie, the nineteen-year-old college student you met in chapter 1 who spends a great deal of her time alone? She is so fearful of relationships that she is rarely curious about other people. Because her mother's severe depression threatened to destroy Julie when she was a child, and because she internalized the profound fear that her own hunger would swallow others, she has very little room for curiosity. Julie has spent her life hiding from other people, so it is very difficult for her to develop any curiosity about them.

What might work for Julie would be to build on her deep interest in and comfort with animals. She doesn't find animals threatening, so she is very curious about how they live. She could begin building up her sense of curiosity about other human beings by first focusing on the feelings of closeness and security she's learned through her connections with animals. By reviewing and focusing on the value of feeling so safe with animals due to her intense curiosity about them, she could take some small steps toward allowing herself to become a little more curious about her own species.

Be patient with yourself if you are not readily curious about other people. There are powerful reasons why you haven't been able to protect and develop your natural capacity for curiosity. You will be able to get to the root of some of these obstacles as you work with remembering in Step Two. In the meantime, praise yourself whenever you do notice that you are questioning or wondering about other people's lives.

Developing Awareness of Yourself in Noncouple Relationships

Becoming more aware of yourself in noncouple relationships could help you overcome your challenges with intimacy. Developing your awareness about yourself in how you connect to your friends, family, children, parents, siblings, coworkers, and others is an important part of learning from your successes. As you become increasingly aware of who you are in various relationships, you may see some very consistent patterns or you may notice that you have more varied relational styles depending on the person you're thinking about.

One of my friends is very gentle and calm in relationships with people who need her support like her clients, anxious coworkers, frail elders. But when she is with people who are less vulnerable, her lack of self-confidence can cause her to be somewhat unpredictable and capricious. When it comes to intimate relationships, she gets into very anxious, avoidant patterns. This woman on a date bears little or no resemblance to the woman who is so competent and emotionally available in her relationships with more fragile people.

Exercise

Building Your Awareness Skills

- In your journal, draw three vertical columns. Label the first column heading "Friends and Colleagues"; the second heading should be "Family (Past and Present)"; and the third "Partners (Current and/or Past)."

- Use an alarm clock or stopwatch to time yourself. For three minutes, write as many one-word descriptions as you can, describing yourself in relation to people who fit in column 1. For the next three minutes, do the same exercise for column 2. Then do the same exercise for column 3.

- Circle any words that appear in more than one column. What does this tell you about yourself? Did you notice that any one of these three columns was easier to do than the other two?

- Do this exercise a second time using the same headings for the three columns, but this time, write one-word descriptions that you think the people in each category would use to describe you in your relationships with them.

- Again, circle the words that appear in more than one column. Are these the same words that showed up when you were writing down your self-awareness descriptions? If not, why do you think others don't see you as you see yourself? Are you tougher on yourself than they would be, or do you think you know yourself better than they do?

- Choose one word that you would most like to see showing up in all three columns, no matter who is rating you.

When you begin to think about all you can learn from this multilayered exercise, you can see that this particular area of awareness is huge and that it has the potential to become a little complicated and confusing.

Now, take a short break to do something completely different for at least thirty minutes. When you come back, write a short description of yourself as someone who exhibits some central themes or consistency in how you relate to other people, but also as someone who clearly has some contradictions.

End this part of awareness skill-building by writing an affirmation about your strengths in relationships. At first, doing this may feel a bit silly or even embarrassing, but it will help you to honor what is most important to you across the board. And it will give you a goal to work toward, that is, the ways in which you would like your intimate relationships to change in order to be as successful as your other, less challenging relationships may be. Here's a sample affirmation to use as a model:

Sample affirmation: I like myself most when I am being compassionate toward the people I care about and letting them know that I am really there for them. I will become able to do this in my intimate relationships. I know that with awareness and willingness, I can.

Cultivating Active Awareness

Let's start this process of learning to practice awareness in regard to your intimate relationships by doing an exercise to illustrate what can happen when you become aware of your own natural learning style, or the process that works best for you when you're starting a new project.

Tuning In to How You Learn

Although it may seem tangential to start with a focus on your learning style, it will make a big difference in how successful you are in this whole process. Once you focus your awareness on what works best for you when you face new challenges and changes, you will be better prepared to use your best learning skills in your journey.

For example, do you approach new ways of connecting by first reading and learning through assimilating information, then analyzing yourself through writing and self-reflection? Or will you do better if you involve others right away in your learning process, availing yourself of their ideas and support? Do you like to use visualization to help you imagine how you want things to be? Do you need to try out new things by "doing," rather than reflecting or talking about it? Will you discover that it really helps you to use body awareness to guide you in what is freeing and what is too distressing?

Not everyone learns the same way. The more you become aware of how you learn best, the more you will know about how to cultivate your awareness. Some people like to know everything about how the new task or activity is supposed to be done before they will try it, while others will learn better by trial and error, that is, "learning by doing." Some people are visual learners while others learn through language. Then there are people who are more intuitive or kinesthetic than logical: they learn how to do something through sensing.

Exercise

Didactic, Experiential, or Intuitive? Learning Your Preferences

Focus on a time when you were learning a new skill. Perhaps this learning experience seemed hard or challenging at first, but eventually you gained confidence and competence. To do this exercise, you can center your attention on something recently learned or you can go back to the past, maybe even as far back as childhood. Your new skill might be learning a new recreational activity, like tennis or salsa dancing, or a new spiritual practice like yoga or meditation. It could be a work-related skill involving some new level of computer competence. You could go back to childhood when you learned to swim, ride a bike, sew, or build a tree house.

Take at least five minutes to concentrate on the details of the experience before you begin to use this to develop increased awareness of how you learn.

Here are some guidelines to help you focus:

- Think about the people who may have helped you with your learning experience.
- Think about how your body felt.
- Remember what your emotions felt like.
- Picture what surrounded you in the environment where you learned this skill.

Once you've really grounded yourself in the memory of this experience, write a paragraph or two describing what was most helpful and what was least helpful. What did you need in order to master this new skill? What might have been an obstacle in your learning process? What helped you know that you were beginning to be successful?

If you feel stuck, read the following example to give you a better idea of how this exercise works.

Example: How I Learned to Improve My Tennis Serve: When I began to really try to learn tennis (instead of just attempting to hit the ball back over the net, something I had tried every five years or so), I had the good fortune to find a wonderful teacher, a tennis coach about my own age.

What I remember most about this learning experience was that I felt joyous and free on the tennis court almost from the beginning of participating in the tennis clinics (groups that were working on their tennis skills with the tennis coach). I think this was because the coach, Deedie, was so encouraging in her praise of us all. Every time one of us did something right, she noticed and commented enthusiastically.

My most vivid memory was a private lesson. I had been frustrated by my inability to achieve a good serve. It seemed that I either smacked the ball into the net or else I hit it over the fence, which might have been fine if we had been playing baseball, but was embarrassing on the tennis court.

What changed that day was the way Deedie helped me learn.

She came across the court and stood behind me where she could watch all the details of how I was hitting the ball. Then she stood right beside me and gently guided my arm through the serve, helping my muscles learn the way they were supposed to work. Finally, she pointed to a cloud low in the sky and told me to aim for the cloud as I hit the ball. This seemed counterintuitive to me. If I hit the ball aiming at the cloud, wouldn't I keep hitting it over the fence? Deedie told me to just relax and give this image a try. She stood back and I began to serve. To my astonishment, the ball went smoothly across the net and into the box where I wanted it to go! I was able to do this repeatedly. I was thrilled. Deedie matched my enthusiasm, reinforcing my joy and astonishment when the new serve kept working.

What does this memory teach me about how I learn best? Here are the main ingredients that I have distilled from this example:

1. I learn best when someone else is helping me in a supportive way, using praise rather than criticism.

2. I learn best by having someone show me something by doing it with me, that is, engaging me by "walking through" the fundamentals of the activity rather than simply describing how to do it.

3. I learn through visualization.

4. I learn best when I let go of my rational, skeptical mind and just let myself do something new instead of thinking about all the reasons why it won't work.

5. I learn best when I share my success with someone, giving myself real praise for what I've accomplished and letting my positive emotions reinforce the experience.

6. I learn best when my intuition has reassured me that whoever is helping me is a "safe" person.

Now it's your turn. In your journal, write down your memory of your learning experience and then make a list of what your memory teaches you about your best learning style.

Doing this exercise has just helped you lay the groundwork for increasing your own awareness of your learning style. This will help you choose the best process of transforming your intimate relationships. Keep what you just learned as a reference throughout this process of learning and changing.

Awareness of the Mind-Body Connection

The mind-body connection is increasingly a central focus in a multitude of books, workshops, magazine articles, medical and mental health practices, meditation, yoga, and other spiritual practices. You may have already done a lot of work on increasing your awareness of how your mind and body are powerfully interconnected. Whether you are very familiar with this topic or not, this is an important area in which to enhance your awareness.

As you begin making any major changes in how you think and interact, your body will often know how well you're doing with the transition before your mind does. Your body signals to you when distressing emotions like fear, shame, anger, and anxiety are bubbling up and making you uncomfortable.

Perhaps, like many people, you often don't know what you're feeling in your conscious mind, but your body tells you by creating physical pain, jumpiness, numbness, or gastrointestinal distress. You can also count on your body to let you know when you're starting to get comfortable with a new idea or behavior or interaction. You may feel a pleasant sensation of your muscles relaxing little by little, or an overall sensation of lightness.

Try the next exercise to see how this works for you. If this is a new focus for you, you may want to take some extra time to make notes on what you've just learned. If this concept is already familiar to you, go ahead and do the exercise anyway to see if anything new comes up for you.

Exercise

Your Body Is Wiser Than Your Mind

This is a two-part exercise. Make sure that you do both parts to avoid side effects.

1. Move into a comfortable place where your body and mind feel relaxed. (If you lie down, you may fall asleep, so you might want to do this in a comfortable chair or even while walking very slowly around the room.) Think about something that's going on in your life right now that's really bothering you. Let yourself concentrate on the details of who or what is really disturbing you. Tell yourself that it's okay to briefly focus on this distressing situation or person because you're not going to stay there.

2. Now begin to slowly scan through your whole body as if you were doing a mental X-ray. Notice where in your body you feel the most discomfort. Where do you feel pain or an unpleasant tightening of your muscles or a feeling of jittery jumpiness?

3. Think about what that unpleasant feeling in your body would look like if you drew a picture or a cartoon. What color is the image or scene? What is it doing to your body? (An example would be picturing red-hot knots all tangled up in your belly, because it feels like knots of tension are burning up in there.)

4. Now take that image and see how you can transform it into something very soothing and pleasant. You could turn the knots

into soft, warm ocean waves, releasing the knots, and healing your belly. Stay with that healing, soothing image for as long as you can. Enjoy its details. See if you can actually feel the healing within your body.

What you've just accomplished was to use your awareness of your mind-body connection to inform yourself about the pain and emotional impact of what's been bothering you. You also used that awareness as a healing tool. Easing your belly pain may not resolve the situation, but now you have a new tool to use whenever you need to deal with the same person or situation the next time around. You can tune in to your body, see what's going on emotionally for you, and visualize a healing image to inoculate yourself against the external distress.

Developing your mind–body awareness will also help to improve your intimate relationships. You will be using this form of awareness in Step Three when you actively practice new skills in your connections to others.

The Story You Tell Yourself

We all have certain images of ourselves or stories we tell to ourselves and others about who we are. Usually, this is a combination of who we want to be and who we really are. Sometimes, we also tell the story of ourselves in a very negative light, emphasizing what we can't do, or what we always do wrong, or the mistakes we've made and can't let go of.

Now let's expand your awareness to go both deeper and wider in creating your awareness map of yourself in intimate relationships. This will help you find a new, more useful story about yourself. To begin focusing your awareness of how you characterize yourself in relationships, let's go through the questions that were raised in earlier chapters as you may have begun to think about yourself as a potential distancer:

Exercise

Who You Are in Couple Relationships

In your journal, write a brief answer to each of the following questions:

1. Do you think that you tend to distance in relationships?

2. Have others told you that you back off, disappear, withhold, or otherwise distance yourself from getting close?

3. Do you generally avoid intimate relationships?

4. Do you prefer intimate relationships in which there's no expectation of commitment?

5. Do you change partners frequently, never really finding what you're looking for in a couple relationship?

6. Are you already moving toward someone new even while you're still in a relationship?

7. Do you go through the motions of being in a committed relationship but feel as though you're not fully present?

8. Do you fear or avoid being genuinely close sexually?

9. Do you keep yourself so busy that there's never enough time to give to your couple relationship?

10. Do you feel that people expect too much of you and that their needs always seem to pull you under?

You have already been considering these questions as you worked with awareness in chapter 1. This time, use your answers to prioritize the issues that are most relevant for you. You can cross out the questions that have little or no relevance for you. Take the questions that remain and consider which ones say the most about you. As you think about these glimpses of yourself, tune your awareness into your body. What's happening inside your body as you think about these matters?

Now take the one or two top questions on your prioritized list. Who else would agree with you about the fit? Would some people be surprised by your self-diagnosis? Would anyone disagree? Again, use your body as a tool to see how this area of awareness makes you feel.

Take notes on all your answers in your journal so you can come back to this and see how it fits with other information you are gathering about yourself. Let's balance any negative thoughts and feelings you might be having about yourself by looking at your relational strengths. In your journal, write brief answers to each question below:

1. Are you a person who is careful about getting into close relationships, taking some time to observe, reflect, and consider whether the other person is likely to bring positive things into your life?

2. Do you have a pretty good intuitive sense about other people, knowing when someone is not necessarily a good fit for you?

3. Do you enjoy solitude and welcome your own company? Do you know how to make the most of your time alone?

4. Do you know how to keep yourself free to pursue activities that really matter to you, such as creative pursuits, platonic friendships, playtime with pets or the children in your life, your spiritual practice, travel, and adventure?

5. Are you able to keep healthy boundaries in close relationships so you don't lose track of who you are and how you're feeling?

6. Do you assert your own preferences and desires when you are sexual with someone?

7. Do you enjoy a wide variety of activities, and give your time generously to family, children, friends, and other relevant communities in your life?

8. Do you know how to be there for others, helping them to feel understood, consoled, and loved?

As you look over your answers to this set of questions, notice if you have cultivated a deeper awareness and appreciation for your strengths. Check out how your body is feeling now.

If you had trouble writing the positive things suggested in the second part of the exercise, remind yourself to come back to this and try again when you have done some more work with yourself and your relationships. Also, you might try asking a trusted friend to go over these questions with you to see if your friend can help you arrive at a more positive awareness of your strengths.

Awareness of Your Favorite Distancing Tactics

Although this area of awareness may seem relatively new to you, in fact, you've probably known for a long time how you create distance between yourself and others. Some of your tactics may be healthy. Others may have been keeping you trapped in confusion, dissatisfaction, frustration, and loneliness. Part of developing more awareness of your distancing tactics involves helping you to decide what to keep and what to let go.

To get started, we're going to use a different part of your brain to access some new information. You will need a few pieces of blank paper and a sharp pencil with an eraser. You will be drawing a kind of diagram to show you how you position yourself in relation to others in certain situations, and to demonstrate visually how you handle discomfort related to your intimate relationships.

Exercise
Drawing Your Favorite Distancing Tactics

Here are some scenes you can draw to aid in obtaining new insights about yourself:

1. Draw yourself and a new love interest during the early stages of starting up a romance. Don't worry about drawing accurate pictures. You can use two circles or a circle and a square to represent how close you two are, whether one of you is chasing the other (label which figure represents you), whether you are surrounded by lots of other people or not (draw more circles or squares), whether you have "happy faces" or are looking scared or angry, whether you're walking off a cliff together or huddled together in a house or under a tree. Is one of the figures moving toward someone else even while the "partner" figure is still in the picture?

2. Use your imagination to draw whatever else you want to represent whatever is most typical for you in a new relationship.

3. Now, try depicting a relationship that is more settled and committed. It could be the relationship you're in now, or one you were once in, or one you imagine yourself being part of in the future.

Notice if the two scenes you drew are very similar or very different. Do you seem to be closer and more comfortable in one picture than the other? Are you the one moving away in both scenes?

By drawing these scenes rather than writing about them or talking, you can obtain a different kind of information. When you use drawing instead of words, you will access a younger and more direct part of yourself. This part is like an "inner child" self who can observe and report the real fundamentals about how you distance. Using adult language qualifies everything and can become so complicated that you may end up not really knowing how to zero in on your primary distancer tactics.

Now, in your journal, write the three most significant things you learned from doing these drawings. Later on, you will refer back to this exercise in self-awareness to see what's changed for you.

Common Distancer Tactics

As you continue to become more and more aware of your inner distancer, keep in mind that you are not the only one. Notice that many people use distancing tactics. Here are some very common ones:

- Blaming the other person
- Avoiding the expression of your feelings
- Pretending that everything is okay when it obviously is not (also called "denial")
- Giving in or giving up (learned helplessness)
- Using addictions to cover up your feelings and keep yourself disconnected
- Using various forms of *dissociation*, which means that you split your mind off from what's really happening so that you aren't really present with the other person, even if you seem to be more or less there
- Filling up your life with lots of other people so there's little or no time left to nurture your couple relationship
- Using jokes and sarcasm to keep others at a distance

As you think about these distancing tactics, think about which tactics you are most likely to use. Try to think of examples in your life that would illustrate these tactics. Write about these in your journal, taking your time to really deepen your awareness of what you've been doing to maintain your loneliness.

Awareness of Community Influences

We are all connected with one another. How you conceptualize and operate in intimate relationships is very much influenced by many levels in your community. There was the family you grew up in, the neighborhood, the schools, your ethnic community, racial, religious, and class identity—all of that just from your childhood.

Then there are all the influences in your adult life. That is, added to the influences that shaped you in childhood, you are also influenced by the people in your life now, the various smaller and larger collections of people or communities that have an impact on your life.

These communities might include your current family or couple relationship, your work or vocational identity, where you live now, who you socialize with, worship with (if relevant), who you attend support groups with, who your friends are, and so forth. Furthermore, there are the very powerful influences of the media: the books or articles you read, the TV shows and movies you watch, the music you listen to and love. All of these are also part of your extended community.

The ideas you've gathered over time about what a couple is supposed to be like are derived from overt messages and less direct influences from all of these parts of your life. It would be a very big task to trace each and every source of your current responses to intimacy as one of a couple, but you can gradually cultivate your awareness of all this at your own manageable pace. The following exercise asks some questions that will help to guide you as you enhance your awareness of these many social and community influences.

Exercise

Awareness of Social and Family Influences

- When you think about what a happy couple would look like, do you picture any couples you know now or you knew earlier in your life? Who are these couples? Are they family members? Are they friends? How would you describe their relationship? (Imagine you are being interviewed by a talk-show host and have only a few minutes to capture the essence of why these two people seem to fit together.)

- Are there fictional couples you identify with on TV or in books or movies? Why do you think you chose these particular couples? In what ways do they represent other couples from the world you identify with now? For example, suppose you've chosen movie stars or other media personalities who seem dedicated to children and family. Is that a strong value that you feel most connected to in your current life? Or is the emphasis on children and family something you've carried with you from childhood? Or perhaps you chose people who seem to lead very exciting lives, traveling and committing themselves to social justice concerns. How does this fit with the values you try to live by? Are these values shared by others who are part of your life now? Were these values part of your life when you were growing up? And what are the values associated with choosing very glamorous people? How does that fit with the other influences in your life?

- Is there a picture in your mind of an ideal couple? What are the ways that this couple reflects the values you grew up with? How is this couple different from the relationships you may have been taught to emulate in childhood?

As you experiment with deepening your awareness in this area of family and social influences, you will find that you can be creative and playful in learning more about yourself. This is also an area where you can invite your partner, or someone you're getting to know, to join you in playing with the couple images this person might choose.

If you do this exercise with your partner, be prepared for the possibility that you may have very different images of the happy or ideal couple from your partner's image. Use this opportunity to practice your new awareness skills of curiosity and mindfulness breathing if you begin to feel upset. Don't jump right into thinking that because you don't share the same picture that there's something wrong with you, or your partner, or that your relationship is doomed.

I once told someone I was dating that my picture of the ideal couple was two people sitting and reading in a cozy living room, a fire going in the fireplace, a cat or two purring. At the same moment, they both look up from their books and smile at each other before they go back to reading. "That's it?!" my new friend asked, going on to say that it sounded distant and boring. Eventually, I recovered from the disappointment I felt, recognizing that we each had very different responses to what my ideal image evoked.

A picture of deep connection and happiness for one person can be another person's nightmare of disconnection and dissatisfaction. The point is to keep talking about it and see where the conversation takes you. For me, the peacefulness of the couple seemed deeply appealing in contrast to my experience of my parents' marriage, and my experience of my least successful couple relationships. The image is a marked contrast to deeply disconnected people who never seem to be in sync with each other.

You can also deepen your awareness of how you are influenced by others in your life by doing some investigating into how others in your life operate as couples.

Exercise

Observing Other People's Beliefs and Behaviors

Use your workplace, or a support group you attend regularly, or any other group of people you spend regular time with (your siblings or other extended family, a volunteer or activity-centered group you're part of) to see if you can recognize and carefully observe another distancer. Choose someone you may identify with and notice how he or she describes an intimate relationship, either past or present. Here are a few examples of the kinds of things you might observe:

Does he or she...

- Blame the significant other for failures in the relationship?
- Mention only superficial events when talking about couple activities (e.g., things they bought together on a shopping trip, or why they liked their rental car on a recent trip they took)?
- Refer to the significant other only when talking about activities involving their children?
- Rarely mention his or her partner?
- Complain often about having to participate in shared activities initiated by the partner? For example, "She dragged me to another play again last weekend" or "I have to go visit his daughter with him again."
- Change the subject when others in the group are talking about special moments they shared with their partner (or a new love interest)?
- Complain that the partner expects too much?

If you are observing a distancer with his or her partner, notice the strategies that you think the distancer uses to avoid intimacy. Observe which strategies he or she appears to employ to prevent being vulnerable or close with his or her partner. Also, pay attention to whether the distancer usually chooses social activities that surround the couple with other people.

After you've completed your observation of the person you think may be a distancer, write a few paragraphs about why you think that, and what you think may have influenced how that person thinks about intimacy and couple dynamics. Do you think that you and this other distancer have been influenced by some of the same familial or social/cultural beliefs and customs? How do you think the two sets of influences may have been different?

As you think about what's had the most influence on your thinking about being in a couple relationship, you will become more aware of some issues than others. Although you can't uncover all such issues at any one time in your life, it will be useful to see which ideas remain the most prominent as you continue to develop your awareness.

Awareness of Fear, Anxiety, and Loss

The distancer's biggest enemy is fear: the fear of mental and emotional pain. Learning to gently deepen your awareness will allow you to get beyond your fear and begin to work with issues that may have caused you years of emotional and mental pain.

In this last part of your awareness work, you are simply encouraged to accept the idea that you need to face some of those emotions and memories that you may have successfully avoided facing in the past by means of denial or dissociation. Don't worry—you won't be forced to excavate old wounds and dive down into your deepest fears, anxieties, or losses. This is just a gentle wake-up call to remind you that by gradually becoming more aware of your uncomfortable areas of experience, you won't have to keep working so hard to keep pain in its cage and eventually you will begin to feel less lonely.

Awareness of the Painful Past

Your ideas about love and couple relationships were undoubtedly very much influenced by your childhood relationships as well as by your past and present couple relationships. These powerful influences usually carry a mixture of gifts and challenges.

Avoidance, on the other hand, is rarely a gift; it is very hard work. Keeping a tight lid on disturbing emotions and memories and trying to ignore your fear of loss can use up enormous amounts of mental and emotional energy, and the stress is bad for your health. Awareness can replace avoidance, both in regard to past pain and in being open to any painful parts of a current relational experience.

Some distancers got so hurt in their early, formative relationships that it made them skeptical and anxious about ever opening their hearts again. In doing this work with awareness, you can make use of your past painful experiences as a teacher, instead of trying so hard to avoid them.

Reviewing and Restorying Old Wounds and Losses

The part of your brain that functions at the primitive level of self-protection can keep you fearful at a completely unconscious level. You probably have many layers of reasons for distancing, yet you may be conscious of painful early experiences only at the more sophisticated, language-based layers of awareness. By working with mindfulness, and learning from the mind-body connection, along with *restorying* (that is, retelling your stories) of your past experiences, you can begin to develop the level of awareness that allows you to make sense of what has been feeding your inner distancer.

Understanding why you feel fear is the first step to being able to let go and take new risks. Cultivating awareness around fears and anxieties will help you understand more about what may be keeping you from finding authentic happiness in your relationships. Facing past (and possible future) losses is a step into the awareness that everything changes, no matter what you might do to try to deny that, and that therefore you know, at your deepest cellular level, that there is nothing that you cannot get through.

Janine's Story

For too long, Janine's fears, anxieties, and the loss of her social network made her avoid anything that could possibly pierce those layers of pain. She stayed encased in a great cocoon of denial. She pushed her awareness of her emotional and mental suffering deep underground into her unconscious by trying to feel nothing at all. She used food as her drug, eating addictively until she ate herself into a stupor of numbness.

It was her sister's intervention around Janine's weight-related diabetes that forced Janine to withdraw from the cocoon of denial and go to the women's center for help. When she began to participate in the trauma and addiction support groups there, she started to glimpse the possibility of allowing some light to enter her shrouded world.

Janine entered the process of cultivating her awareness by learning mindfulness breathing, becoming aware of the intricate relationship between her mind and her body, and finally beginning to believe that she could get beyond the pain of her past.

She used her newly acquired awareness of the family and cultural influences that had caused her to feel such shame about her victimization; slowly she began to see that the lack of support she'd been given by the people who supposedly loved her derived from a place of ignorance. Their callousness had been caused by their lack of awareness, their lack of consciousness, not because they had stopped loving her.

Finally, Janine was ready to move toward awareness of fear, pain, and grief, taking slow little steps, one at a time. There was no magic formula for doing this. It was just the way it is for everyone else who has been running from pain. She let awareness enter slowly, sharing her experience with others who knew what it felt like and were able to offer her true empathy and compassion. As she worked through the remembering process of Step Two, she learned that she could finally put all the pieces together and gain enough confidence to try out the new connections she would make doing the work of Step Three.

Now that you are moving forward to do the work of Step Two, the next task is to understand the factors that most influenced your approach to relationships. You will discover that the roots of pain also contain the strength of resilience. Now, take a deep breath, and step through the next door.

3 Step Two, Part One: Learning from Childhood

You are about to begin Step Two, which is remembering the roots of your distancing patterns. Some of the early experiences that shaped you may be as clear in your mind as the stones in a clear stream, while other important relationships and situations may have been tucked away in the deepest recesses of your memory. In this chapter, as we work with the past, you will slowly extricate yourself from the quicksand of painful old memories. We will explore the past carefully, going back just long enough to uncover the mysteries of your current relationships.

Step Two is a two-step process. First, in this chapter, we will focus on the people and events in your childhood that created the roots of your distancing. Then, in chapter 4, we'll move on to examine the key aspects of the relationships in your adult life that have brought you to this point in your relational journey.

Looking at Childhood for Sources of Relationship Patterns

There are many roots for distancing. There are ghosts, past experiences of being wounded or betrayed that may play a major role in your need for distance. Past experiences may have led to defensiveness, anxiety, or fear; combative behaviors like excessive joking or sarcasm; or being very judgmental. Childhood experiences may have caused you to fear that you could lose your self, your identity, your autonomy, or your freedom of self-expression. You may fear the loss of your independence because as a child you had too many responsibilities (for example, caring for alcoholic or emotionally impaired parents). Being in a committed relationship may frighten you because you fear losing your economic independence; as a child, you may have watched helplessly while the adults in your life lost housing, jobs, or dignity because of their love relationships.

You may have had childhood experiences that planted the seeds of ambivalence, the belief that there's always something better out there waiting—the "grass is always greener" anywhere but in the relationship you're just getting into or just getting out of. There may be ancient subterranean rivers of anxiety within you that fuel your current spinning as a "crisis junkie." Maybe you cannot focus on a partner because you get hooked by every little daily life drama; for example, a friend's marital problems, your cat getting into a minor skirmish with the cat next door, or your indecision about whether to attend your cousin's birthday party or your neighbor's annual June barbecue.

The Only Way Out Is the Path Through

While the ARC (Awareness, Remembering, and Connecting) model emphasizes learning new insights and skills to help you change your present to a better one, you can't arrive at a healthy present without understanding the past. During my own recovery and the healing experiences I've shared with friends and clients, I've learned there are some very good reasons to take the sometimes difficult trip back through the past.

Refusing to remember is a trap that keeps us stuck in old, unnecessary dysfunctional patterns. I remember watching my mother put on her "happy" face; she avoided painful memories by stating proudly "I remember only the good things." She paid a steep price for her embrace of denial.

Below are some reasons to choose awareness over denial:

Self-Knowledge Is Power

You have a choice: you don't have to be the victim of loneliness. You can take charge of your present-day relationships by using your awareness and your knowledge of the past. Remembering and understanding the lessons of the past will give you much more control over how you choose to act in the present.

Remembering Stops Painful Repetition

Remembering and getting to the root of your relationship issues can save you from repeating the same mistakes. You can actually choose to avoid that moment when you suddenly realize you have become your mother or father.

Remembering Increases Compassion

While you are piecing together all that comprises the root of your current relationship patterns, you will begin to steadily increase your compassion for yourself. You will also gain more compassion for your significant others, both past and present. Feeding compassion is like feeding a growing child: nurturance is required, but the rewards are immeasurable. Compassion is the best antidote to the poison of self-hatred and resentment toward others.

Remembering Strengthens Your Capacity for Change

The more you are able to remember and analyze your past, the more you can enrich and expand the complex story of who you are. As you become aware of the full richness and texture of your story, you will become more hopeful about your capacity to change. Those who get stuck in the rut of endless unhappiness are often trapped in an oversimplified view of themselves: Telling yourself that you "just can't do relationships" is sentencing yourself to self-imprisonment. Such a prison is built on a foundation of ignorance, the refusal to examine the past.

Understanding Your Own Roots Increases Your Understanding of Others

The more you can learn about your past's influence in shaping your current relationships, the more you will understand the other person in your current couple relationship, or the person you left, or the one who got away. Your increased capacity to understand the past is such a valuable tool because it allows you to recognize and understand that relationship challenges are neither all your fault nor all your responsibility.

Remembering Helps You to Prioritize Your Areas of Challenge

Let's say that you've recognized that you were most negatively affected by your parents' alcoholic marriage and their emotional neglect of you. When doing Step Two work, you might decide the most important change you can make would be to decrease your workaholic patterns in order to stop distancing from your partner. You might realize that you don't want to be missing in action from your marriage, the way that your parents' alcoholism prevented them from connecting emotionally with each other. Prioritizing your relational challenges means you are successfully using your memories to improve your current relationships.

"But I've Already Overanalyzed the Past..."

You may have been told that you've already spent more than enough time remembering your past and analyzing it. Many kinds of recovery treatments do direct people to stay away from their painful pasts and focus on learning new skills and new ways of retraining the brain. Even trauma experts currently place less focus on remembering and more emphasis on learning to cope in the present.

In the work you'll be doing with the ARC model, however, you'll find that there are ways to revisit the past without having to relive it. If we just wade into our past painful memories without the necessary swimming skills, we can easily drown or be pulled into treacherous quicksand. We need to know how to touch down lightly, looking at what shaped us long enough to understand it. We don't need to move back into memory's house of ghosts and monsters.

Even if you have spent a substantial amount of time already examining your past, Step Two will give you new tools and new goals. Working with Step Two is like taking a class in which you are the subject, and you are the expert. You are enrolling in a self-study course and you determine your schedule. You can choose to pace yourself. Take a break anytime you feel yourself slipping back into old feelings of anxiety, shame, depression, anger, or fear.

Exercise

Explore Your Resistance

Now that you've been introduced to some of the reasons to revisit your past by going into it—not around it—you can ready yourself for Step Two by doing this exercise. It will help you examine any resistance you may have to remembering your past, so that you can go on to Step Two with increased willingness.

Part One: Here are some questions to help you look at your personal roadblocks:

1. What would tempt you to skip over your past and go directly to Step Three?

2. Who would tell you to avoid looking at your past?

3. Who would urge you to dig into your memories?

Take a few minutes to write your answers in your journal. Then we'll move into the second part of the exercise.

Part Two: By thinking about who would urge you to skip over your past, you deepen your awareness of the influences that may have most affected your past choices. Visualize these influences being erased from your mental screen so that you can concentrate on what you need to do. Practice tuning in to your awareness of those people who would be your best supporters. Picture these people cheering you on, or shaking your hand to congratulate you, or beckoning to you to join them at the finish line of your personal marathon.

If you start to feel disloyal to the family you grew up with, here are some tips on how to let go of your guilty feeling. Remembering doesn't mean that you have to judge or condemn or expose any of the people or events from your childhood. You are simply observing what happened and noticing how this influences your current relationships. You're not blowing the whistle and you're not blaming others. You're just examining the past in order to construct a happier life for yourself in the present.

Seeds of Resilience Within the Painful Past

You don't have to focus exclusively on the painful parts of your relational legacy. You must also learn to honor the strengths you gained from your early experiences. Here's the buried treasure, the essence of why we do the work of Step Two. Write the following slogan in your journal, and come back to it as often as you need to:

Within our vulnerabilities lie the seeds of our strength.

Despite having endured a very painful childhood, I discovered the truth of the famous maxim "that which doesn't kill you makes you stronger." I was tormented by my father's sexual and physical assaults. But he had other qualities I loved, especially his endless repertoire of bedtime stories. My father's stories actually helped me survive the craziness of his abuse. Not only did the stories transport me far away from what was happening in the darkness of my bedroom, but I delighted in a world of fantasy where anything was possible.

Although I was unquestionably harmed by my father's nighttime visitations, I was also inspired by the adventures my father created for me. In these stories, my father created an ever-continuing hero's tale in which I was a brave little ship's captain, navigating a magical journey in my Noah's Ark, which was filled with whimsical animals who were free to become anything they chose.

Fortunately, the day came when I escaped my father's abuse. I was no longer silent. I began to tell stories of my own. The telling of these stories gradually released me from shame and isolation. Eventually, I learned to heal myself by creating a world in which I was a whole, powerful, and joyous being. Only then did my identity change from that of a victim trapped in helplessness to that of a whole person with a large repertoire of responses and emotions.

All human beings can learn to heal through hearing the stories of others. Stories of others who also had difficult childhoods showed me I was not alone, and gave me the courage to throw off the shackles of victimhood.

No matter what kinds of childhood experiences shaped who you are today, there are ways to honor the positive significance of your experiences by understanding their power to make you stronger, smarter, more resilient in mind, body, and spirit. There are skills to learn: new ways to think, new awareness to cultivate about how your mind and body work together to heal and strengthen. And, finally, new capacities will emerge as a direct response to difficult past experiences that offer the promise of relating to other people in a deeper, more joyful way.

The Five Major Roots of Distancing

There are five major clusters of childhood experience that most often generate distancing patterns in adult relationships. They are as follows:

1. **Dysfunctional parental marriages,** marked by constant conflict, scarring betrayals, or chronic disengagement

2. **Inadequate parents or caregivers,** who were impaired by substance abuse, mental or physical illness, or personality disorders

3. **Loss,** of a parent to death, loss of the original parental unit to divorce, loss of home or community to family misfortune or community disasters

4. **Neglect,** as evidenced by grossly inadequate nurturance, the absence of parental attention and affection, or inadequate basic material resources (clothing, health care, personal possessions)

5. **Abuse,** including physical, psychological, and sexual abuse

To help you figure out what were the most significant formative influences from your childhood, here are some illustrations for each of these five categories that tell the stories of other distancers:

Unhappy Marriages as Formative Models

The most obvious root of problems with intimate relationships is attributable to growing up with unhappily married parents. Whether or not the marital misery culminated in divorce, the atmosphere created by an unhappy marriage has a very strong negative impact on how the children of that marriage grow into their adult relationships. As a rule, unhappy marriages are characterized by frequent conflicts between parents, or betrayals (affairs are the most common), or simply a passionless, disengaged, "dead" marriage.

Andrew's Story

Andrew had a number of negative challenges as a child. His father was an alcoholic, his older brothers were verbally abusive, and his

mother spent more time at church than with her family. But as I continued getting to know him, it became clear that the most difficult challenge Andrew faced was the model of his parents' marriage. His hyperanxiety might have been generated by the unpredictability of his father's alcoholism, but his fear of intimate relationships went straight to the core issue, the marriage he had witnessed throughout his childhood. His memories of this powerfully negative relationship controlled him on a deeply unconscious level.

Andrew had grown up observing a distant, passionless marriage. His father was lost in the bottle and his mother was hidden in the priest's confessional booth. Andrew was able to talk easily about both his father's alcoholism and the verbal violence inflicted on him by his brothers, but he was oblivious to the impact of how his parents' marriage had affected him. "Why didn't your mother leave your father when she couldn't bear his drinking any longer?" I asked Andrew at one of our early meetings.

He looked back at me in astonishment. "How could she leave?" he asked. "My mother was a good Catholic woman. Nobody in my family ever got divorced. It just wasn't an option."

It became clearer and clearer that at the very core of Andrew's being, there was still a frightened child afraid to be trapped as his mother and his father had been. On an unconscious level, he believed that if he just kept moving fast enough he would not end up in a loveless prison.

Chris's Story

Chris, on the other hand, was very conscious of how negative her parents' marriage had been and how their conflicts had led to their inevitable divorce. She thought she had found an escape hatch by partnering with a gentle, nurturing woman, but, in fact, Chris had entered the same unhappy prison of a conflicted relationship. Her refusals to communicate her feelings directly was just another route to an unhappy relationship. She and Beth were almost as miserable as her parents had been, even if she couldn't see that at first.

In couples therapy, Chris resisted comparing her ten-year relationship with Beth to her parents' marriage, which had finally culminated in a bitter divorce. "I'm not getting where you're going with this," she said to me indignantly. "My parents were so unhappy, they got a divorce. Beth and I have made our relationship work for ten years. There's not really anything that wrong with us. We don't even fight! My parents were always yelling at each other. You just don't get it!"

After a few more frustrating couples therapy sessions, Beth began to fear that she and Chris were headed down the same road that Chris's parents had taken. Beth said, "If Chris doesn't learn how to open up with me, I don't know if I can stick around much longer. It might be better if we did a little yelling ourselves—at least there would be some emotions in the room. Now, it's like we're living in an isolation tank or something with no color and no sound."

Chris would remain stuck in an emotional twilight zone until she became able to see where her fear of conflict had begun.

Inadequate Parents and Caregivers

Many distancers grew up with parents or other caregivers who were impaired by substance abuse, mental disorders, physical illnesses, or personality problems that caused them to be very self-centered, needy, or wildly unpredictable. The impact of such impairment on children can appear to be quite diverse, but most children raised by inadequate parents become adults with deeply entrenched fears of becoming stuck in a permanent caretaker role. Or they engage in excessive caretaking to the detriment of all other aspects of their adult relationships.

Ben's Story

Ben couldn't get really close to a partner without quickly becoming overwhelmed by his ambivalence and his need to flee. He was the older son of an unhappy, needy mother, and an absent, workaholic father. His younger brother had struggled with serious mental illness throughout his life, and avoided most opportunities for intimacy. Ben had been deeply affected by the emptiness of his parents' marriage.

Ben's mother had lived vicariously through Ben for as long as he could remember. She suffered from chronic disappointment and dissatisfaction in her marriage, as well as most aspects of her life. Because Ben's father was unavailable due to his workaholism, Ben's mother sought to meet her emotional needs through her bond with Ben and his younger brother.

"I never felt that I had a life of my own," Ben says, describing his mother's hunger to be included in all aspects of her older son's existence. "She needed me to experience everything that she couldn't have for herself, so I always felt the pressure to be out there in the world living life for her. But at the same time, I was always getting the message to never leave her."

Needless to say, Ben lacked any opportunity to observe a close loving relationship between two adults. He described feeling suffocated at times by his mother's emotional needs. His response, over time, had been to pull back each time he started to get close to a potential partner. In this way, he avoided the possibility of anyone needing him, threatening to suffocate him, or trying to take over his life. His ambivalence for each new partner, enacted by always finding flaws that allowed him to escape, was a continuing act of loyalty and submission to his mother. By never really committing to a relationship, Ben never left his mother for another woman.

Julie's Story

Julie, the young woman who avoids relationships entirely, traces the roots of her distancing back to the shame she felt because her mother was severely depressed when she was a child. Julie had learned to stay distant from others because she was working overtime to conceal her mother's emotional disorder. Living in a childhood emotional fortress constructed by shame, she didn't have the opportunity to practice normal boundary-setting around the issues of closeness and distance. Her adult choice to continue walling herself off from close relationships is rooted both in shame and fear.

Colin's Story

Colin, the alcoholic lawyer who drives women away, can't stop sabotaging his intimate relationships. His alcoholism is certainly a precipitating factor in his failed romances, but it is a symptom rather than the root of the problem. Colin's childhood helps to explain why he is so dramatically split between the kindness and generosity his colleagues and clients see and the harsh, raging behavior he exhibits in intimate relationships.

Colin was the casualty of a rejecting mother and a passive, helpless father. He may have been an only child, but Colin was not the stereotypical little prince cherished by adoring parents. He was an unwanted and unloved child whose mother let him know that he was the cause of her ruined life. She had been in her first year of nursing school when she accidentally conceived Colin in a one-night fling with his father, a retail store manager she'd met at a bar. She never allowed Colin or his father to forget how her life had been derailed by Colin's arrival.

His mother's self-centered lack of affection for Colin was to some extent mediated by his father who was genuinely fond of his son. Unfortunately, his father was thoroughly intimidated by his wife's angry, contemptuous attitude toward him and his son. Colin grew up to be as harsh and contemptuous toward the women in his life as his mother had been toward him and his father.

Although Colin admits he can see the connection between his sarcasm and hostility and the way he was treated as a child, he has not yet been able to end his cycle of relational misery. It is interesting that his best characteristics come into play at his job. As a successful attorney, he has made something of himself through his work, accomplishing more than either his father or mother could.

Childhood Losses

Loss can have as much of an impact on children as abuse or neglect. Traumatic losses can include the death or disappearance of a parent (or primary caregiver); the loss of home or community, which occurs when children are removed from their parents; or losses caused by economic circumstances, natural disasters, political upheavals, or war. Less dramatic, but nonetheless significant, losses can have a lifetime impact on the child who loses a special role in the family when a younger sibling comes along, or when stepchildren join the family. Childhood losses can easily go underground, yet they can become major causes of troubled relationships in adult life.

Diego and Luisa

Even though Diego and Luisa may seem to be very different in their distancing patterns, they shared the experience of having gone through major childhood losses.

Luisa's losses were much more visible than Diego's. She had grown up in Cuba, but when her parents emigrated to the United States, she lost her country, her language, her community, her childhood home, and her culture. Unlike many other Cuban exiles, Luisa's family did not relocate to a community of other Cuban exiles. Instead, they moved to Massachusetts where they experienced profound cultural alienation.

Luisa's parents taught her to look down on everyone in their predominantly Puerto Rican community, and she experienced rejection by the Anglo children who dominated the private Catholic school she attended. Luisa became very cautious and controlled in everything she did, trying to hold on to whatever she could, to give herself a marginal sense of security.

Diego was more fortunate in his community surroundings. Although his young, single mother was very poor, Diego felt at home in his neighborhood and extended family. His loss occurred suddenly, as the result of what would seem to be a nontraumatic natural event. When he was six, his mother gave birth to his younger sister, Lourdes, and Diego's life turned upside down. He had been the center of his mother's attention for every minute he could remember of his first six years; he had felt completely loved and adored. When he was suddenly displaced by his sister, the intruder, he was devastated.

Due to the overwhelming stresses of poverty, Diego's mother had been unable to make the transition from adored only child to mere older brother less traumatic for her six-year-old son. Baby Lourdes had required extra care because she was a poor eater, poor sleeper, and, generally, just a very sensitive infant. Diego had experienced a sense of crushing abandonment and emptiness where there had always been boundless maternal attention and affection.

He became convinced that he was defective in some profound way. His childhood loss became the wound that fueled his adult need for emotional reassurance and sexual healing. Once the honeymoon phase with Luisa ended, he felt abandoned and rejected once again, without really understanding where these feelings had originated.

Luisa's distancing, through her need to keep emotions tightly wrapped, led her to require her marriage to remain very tightly controlled and orderly. Diego's emotional volatility disturbed her and seemed unmanly. They became as estranged as if they were from two different planets.

Danny's Story

Danny, the talented science-fiction writer, suffered a traumatic loss when his mother died while he was only twelve. He was a lost adolescent with no one available to take the place of his warm, loving mother. His older brother and his father were too wounded by their own loss to be able to help him. He retreated from close relationships, and found comfort in the science-fiction world he created. On the surface he seemed surprisingly resilient, enjoying precocious success at fifteen when he published his first sci-fi story. He published his first science-fiction novel when he was twenty-five and the second one a few years later.

Danny was not only a successful writer, he was also handsome, charming, and happy in the company of his friends, his father, and his brother. His loneliness was hidden at a deep level where he longed for a fulfilling, passionate relationship. He had dated the same woman for several years, but never quite managed to spend enough time with her to deepen their connection. Sex was fun, but infrequent. They'd never discussed living together, and often went weeks at a time without seeing each other. As gifted as he was, Danny was clueless about how to change his life and equally clueless about the roots of his distancing.

Neglect, the Hidden Culprit

Neglect is manifested by the absence of parental love, attention, or caretaking. There are many forms of childhood neglect. The failure to attend to a child's emotional life is a form of neglect that is far too common. Neglect can and does occur in very rich families, as well as in families that are overwhelmed by poverty.

Too often, childhood neglect is overlooked as a very important contributor to chronic problems in adult life. Whether it's discussed on a talk show or in a psychotherapy office, childhood abuse tends to get everyone's attention. However, there are many people who were as deeply wounded by various forms of childhood neglect as the survivors of childhood abuse were, but this kind of childhood pain is generally not perceived as traumatic. In my work with people who struggle with addictions, compulsions, and self-sabotaging relationships, I've seen that the neglect factor can play a major role in their current challenges.

Janine's Story

Janine's childhood was one, long continuous experience of never being supported or viewed as a valuable, lovable person. She grew up with her mother and her mother's series of boyfriends as the fifth of six siblings. She was close to her younger sister, but her older siblings had survived their childhoods by being out of the home as much as possible. Janine had suffered the neglect of not being given the attention a child needs to develop self-esteem and the sense of being loved. She also received very little support in learning how to care for her body, or help with developing the skills necessary for self-protection.

Janine's experience of pervasive neglect was clearly amplified by the trauma of being raped. Her way of internalizing the neglect was to become very isolated and to try to soothe and comfort herself through overeating. Both her isolation and her food addiction kept her in a distancing pattern until she began to share some of herself in the women's group.

Sally's Story

Sally was astonished when I suggested to her in our therapy sessions that she had been traumatized by childhood neglect. I explained to her that I thought she had been emotionally neglected. She shook her head and looked at me warily. "I think you must be thinking of another client," she said.

I assured Sally that I was remembering her descriptions of childhood. "I think you were neglected, Sally," I continued gently. "The neglect took place during the years when your parents were always moving your family; when sometimes your father suddenly made a lot of money, and then the next month he had to sell all the furniture in the house to make ends meet. Also, I think you were neglected when your mother was physically ill so often, and when your younger sister's emotional problems became your problem. I don't think there was much time or space for you to get the adult love and attention every child needs."

"But I always knew my parents loved me," Sally countered. "It was chaotic and unpredictable, but I had enough to eat, I had nice clothes, I had a home. I was part of a close, loving family. How could I have been neglected?"

It took some time for Sally to become aware of how little attention she had received as a child. She had to look back at how quickly she had been forced into the role of the oldest child, the one who was expected to be endlessly competent, who was supposed to look out for the younger kids, and to be emotionally available for her siblings whenever her mother came down with another of her many physical illnesses.

Child Abuse

In today's society, we are exposed to what feels like an epidemic of child abuse. We now know that not only little girls but also little boys are frequently sexually abused. We have always known that both boys and girls are physically abused too often by their parents and other primary caregivers. Verbal abuse, that is, constant criticism or shaming, is another pervasive form of child abuse. Finally, we are becoming more aware of the impact that witnessing physical abuse and violence has on children. All over the world children are routinely traumatized by the violence that they see all around them.

Experiencing any form of abuse can create a broad spectrum of responses in the adult. Survivors of violence and abuse can grow up to be relatively okay adults. Survival depends on how the child perceives his or her role in the abusive relationship, how secretive the child is forced to be, how young the child is, and most of all, the level of protection and support the child experiences in the aftermath of abuse.

As you read this last group of stories, you may find that you are especially disturbed by them, especially if you are a survivor of abuse yourself. Remember to take breaks from reading or thinking about this if you need to. Make use of the breathing and other relaxation skills you learned in chapter 2.

Yvonne's Story

Yvonne had been sexually abused by her older brother for many years. They never spoke about the abuse; not during the years it was going on and never in the many years that followed. Yvonne did make an early attempt to disclose what was going on when the abuse first began, choosing her father as her confidant. But he became enraged with her, denying that his adored only son could possibly do such a thing.

Yvonne's mother had left the family when Yvonne was eight, abandoning her children and her husband. After her mother left, Yvonne's father and brother became strong allies. Her father came to depend more and more on his son while he raged and grieved the sudden departure of his wife. Yvonne was harmed both by the traumatic loss of her mother and the sexual demands of her brother. She felt helpless and confused, especially by her father's denial and rage when she tried to get his help. He made her feel that she herself was dirty and disgusting, and that a girl her age must be "twisted" to come up with such a story.

It is certainly not surprising that when Yvonne began her relationship with her boyfriend, she dreaded being sexual with him and stayed as distant from him as possible by not telling him anything about what was going on for her.

Rick's Story

Rick was sexually abused by his parish priest off and on when he was an altar boy. He guessed the abuse was also happening to other boys in the parish, but he thought he was the only one to sometimes enjoy the physical aspects of the experience. However, he was ashamed, even horrified, by the sexual pleasure he experienced, and when he became a teenager, he worked hard at becoming a strong, powerful football star, and when he joined the military, he became one tough soldier.

It wasn't until he was an adult with a wife and children that the scandals about the clergy's sexual abuse of children began to surface all around him. Still, he told no one, keeping his secret with the same crippling shame he had felt as a young boy. In his marriage, his overcompensating, controlling style was rooted in his experience of being sexually used by an adult male who was supposed to represent safety and goodness.

Family Violence

Family violence, much like child neglect, often receives little attention when the adult brings life problems into the therapy office. Yet many people, especially those with chronic relationship issues, were deeply affected by family violence when they were growing up. Physical and emotional abuse is committed by fathers and mothers and by older siblings. Such abuse creates lasting traumatic emotional scars, especially when it is severe, chronic, and/or sadistic.

The victim of family violence may develop patterns in his or her adult relationships that mirror the behavior of the original abuser or reproduce the child's fearfulness and compliance. Adult survivors of family violence may use a threatening, aggressive style to maintain distance when they are in a couple relationship, or else they may distance by seeming to accommodate their partner's wishes and needs (while actually absent at the deeper levels of emotional connection).

Jack's Story

Jack (Diane's on-again off-again partner) was the kind of distancer who always seemed to be dancing a relational tango: dancing toward his beloved and then reversing his direction to move backwards halfway through the dance. As long as he remained in this relational tango, he never got close enough to emotionally embrace his partner and to create a meaningful union.

His distancing behavior was rooted in his childhood experience of being physically abused by his violence-prone father. He was also scarred by the amount of violence he witnessed. Both as the victim of his father's battering and the witness to many other acts of violence in his family, it was not surprising that Jack was in denial about his adult relational reenactments of his childhood with rejecting partners. Not only did he replay the victim role from his abused childhood, but he himself was a well-disguised distancer. On the surface, he looked like the good guy who really wanted to be with his rejecting partner, but, in fact, his hidden distancing only proved the point that "it takes two to tango"!

Finding the Right Fit

After you've read about these various root causes of adult distancing, it's possible that the roots of your own distancing don't seem to fit into any of the categories just covered. No one size fits all, so, not finding yourself described in any of the categories discussed above is a valid response. We are all experts on our own stories.

To shed some light on the roots of your own distancing, you might find it useful to ask a few others you know, that is, people who seem to you to be distancers, whether they had some of the same or similar experiences in their childhoods that you've identified in yours. There is no reason to try to squeeze yourself into a category that isn't right for you. We are all individuals with our own unique paths from childhood to where we are now. As you work on remembering the roots of your distancing, the situations described above will most likely touch on your own and be helpful to you, even if they don't precisely match your own situation.

From Past to Present: Working with Your Memories

You may not realize it, but you may have already started working hard on Step Two. While you were reading about other distancers and reviewing their various childhood experiences, you probably began the work of remembering your own childhood experiences. If you've done that, you've probably begun to make connections with those stories and experiences that are most like yours. This is similar to the work on awareness and self-identification that you did in Step One when you were locating yourself among the various styles of distancing.

Getting Started

You're going to continue to use your tools of awareness and self-analysis. Also, you're going to experience some turbulence, so we will continue developing tools to help you manage any disturbing feelings that arise. You will be able to use your past to strengthen, not to debilitate, yourself.

Now, here's a checklist to use to remind yourself of the most common childhood influences in the relationship patterns of adult distancers:

- Growing up with unhappily married parents as your role model. They may have been parents who were embroiled in frequent, unresolved conflicts; parents who were extremely disconnected from each other; or parents who were injured by betrayals or constant put-downs or contemptuous attitudes from their spouses.

- Growing up with impaired parents, that is, parents who were unable to provide basic affection, attention, and caregiving because of substance abuse or other addictions; or because of emotional and psychological problems such as depression or narcissism; or because of chronic physical illness; or because they were struggling with the realities of poverty, immaturity, or single-parent overload.

- Being impacted by traumatic losses, for example, the death or disappearance of one parent; the loss of home, community, or extended family due to political upheaval, natural disaster, or job loss; or the sudden loss of parental attention when a new child enters the family or when parents find a new partner.

- Being impacted by neglect, for example, not being provided with basic adult attention or affection, or material necessities; or being emotionally neglected.

- Being impacted by family violence, for example, being battered or witnessing other family members being physically abused; being psychologically battered through being yelled at, blamed, constantly criticized, or treated with contempt.

- Being sexually abused, for example, being sexually molested by a parent or other adult caregiver, or an older sibling, or a trusted person in the community; or witnessing the sexual abuse of other children.

It's Not All Bad News

There really is no point in going back to relive painful memories unless you can work with your past to build a better present. We don't always get that message. There are still many talk shows, reality shows, books, and feature articles that shine the spotlight on someone's suffering as though suffering is a form of entertainment. Note that, as you begin to compare your story with the stories of other distancers, it's important to understand that your painful experiences may have had a negative impact but, most likely, they also created some of your strengths and special gifts.

Here are a few positive aspects to remembering difficult childhood experiences:

- When you don't get everything you need, the deprivation can help you become very resourceful. You learn some great survival skills, like not passively waiting for someone else to provide for you.

- When you are pushed into a place where you have to keep yourself alert to avoid being hurt, you often develop excellent observation skills and survival instincts. You tend to see what's going on around you faster than those who grew up protected by the adults in their lives.

- If you witnessed a lot of dysfunctional behavior, it may have helped you learn how to avoid potentially harmful situations and people.

- If you grew up with abusive or impaired parents, it may have strengthened your determination to be healthier in your own adult life.

- If you grew up having to take care of your parents, you may have some very valuable skills as a listener, caretaker, provider, and counselor. (It's hard to find a dedicated mental health provider who grew up in a healthy family!)

- If you felt unsafe with people as a child, you may have developed a very special relationship with nature, animals, books, art, music, sports, and so forth. Childhood suffering created many people whose self-reliance resulted in extraordinary achievements. It also created many people who are content engaging in solitary activities like reading, exploring outdoors, being an artist, or doing scientific research.

You may have many more strengths you are not aware of because of having been less fortunate than other children in how you were nurtured and raised. Keep in mind that *within our vulnerabilities lie the seeds of our greatest strengths.*

Step Two can be emotionally charged, so make sure that you do the following exercises at a time when you can bring yourself back to the present moment and keep living the rest of your daily life. Although there's some truth to the slogan "no pain, no gain," you don't need to retraumatize yourself to do this work. Choose a time of day when you can talk to someone, or go for a walk, or watch a movie, or do anything else that would be soothing if doing the exercises stirs up too much intensity. Going back in time is difficult work when you're looking at painful experiences. Proceed at a safe pace and use your favorite self-soothing practices to protect yourself. Keep in mind that you are no longer a child, and you have choices that you didn't have back then.

Exercise

Practicing Detachment

This is a warm-up exercise designed to help you remind yourself that you can take charge of your memories. You can use them to help you create better relational experience in the present, but you don't have to allow them to stir up needless suffering.

First, take a few minutes to relax your body and your mind. Begin to think about something that makes you happy. This could be something as uneventful as putting your feet up and watching a favorite TV show, or going for a walk with your dog, or making vegetable soup. Take the time to visualize all the details of this happy picture. For example, if your happy image is taking a walk with your dog, notice how the air feels. Is it warm or cool? What do you see, hear, and smell? What do you notice that tells you the dog is having a good time too? How does your body feel? Are you smiling? Humming a tune? Talking to your dog?

Second, after you've visualized the happy scene for a few minutes, shift your attention to something in the past week that bothered you. It could be something that happened at work, or something a friend told you, or something at home that annoyed or disappointed you. It could be something you read or saw on the news that upset you.

Then do the same kind of review of the details surrounding this event that you did in the first part of this exercise. Picture your surroundings when you got upset. What kinds of details can you remember? Where were you standing or sitting, what else was going on, who else was present? Also, try to remember if you can how your body felt when you became upset. Were you likely to have experienced discomfort in your shoulders, your gut, your head? Do you remember if your skin got warm? Did your breathing change?

Third, we're going to move back in time now. Allow yourself, without thinking too long about it, to pull up a memory from your childhood, one that isn't really bad or really good—something more or less routine. When you have your memory, anchor its details in your mind using some of the same prompts you used for the first and second parts of this exercise. That is, try to recall the surroundings in your memory. Take a guess at what you and any others might have been wearing.

Now, here comes the really important part of the exercise: Detach yourself from the experience by pretending that you're the cameraman (or woman) filming this event for a movie. See whether you can put yourself inside the mind of this person who just wants to get all the details right. What does the camera see when it films you as a child? Try to get yourself into a place of detachment where you can observe this scene without going back in time and becoming part of it.

After doing this very important piece of work for a few minutes, switch your mind back into the present moment and practice any of the following self-care routines:

- Do some deep breathing (find a really comfortable position) so that you can feel your breath slowing down. This will help you to relax your entire body.
- Do a muscle tension and relaxation exercise: tighten various muscle groups (hands, shoulders, stomach, thighs, face), hold the tension for a count of five, then relax and shake it out.
- Look at pictures that relax or soothe you (for example, scenes from a beach, a brook, farmland, ocean waves).
- Smell an especially pleasant scented candle.
- Listen to some soothing music.

Congratulations! You've just completed a very important piece of work. The purpose of doing this exercise was for you to practice focusing on useful information from your past and learning skills that will help you to access childhood memories without allowing them to pull you back into the pain or distress you may have felt back in childhood when you didn't have the choices you have now. If you had difficulty with this exercise, remind yourself that you can try recalling it again until you begin to feel more confidence in your ability to analyze the past from a detached place.

Avoiding the Fight, Flight, or Freeze Reaction

It's fairly common to react to old memories by lapsing into old, dysfunctional forms of trying to protect yourself. When you were a vulnerable little child, you may have tried to protect yourself from your pain, fear, or anxiety by one of the universal, instinctive responses to danger; that is, fight, flight, or freeze behavior. Now that you're an adult, your tactics of self-protection may not be as obvious as your childhood responses were.

When you were a kid, you may have tried escaping from your situation by running away, hiding, dissociating (so your body or feelings weren't present), going numb, or taking your rage out on another child or yourself. Now that you're an adult, you may find that you try to do the same thing when the distress of old memories triggers your emotions. Here are some of the most common responses to retrieving painful old memories:

1. Indulging in your addiction of choice: You may stuff yourself with food, or stop eating completely; or you may increase your drug or alcohol use; or try to escape through activities like overworking, compulsive shopping, spending too much time in cyberspace, or exercising compulsively.

2. Dissociating: This can include feeling as if you're not really present; developing a quick case of amnesia for what you've just been remembering; shutting down so that you have no feelings at all; getting so confused in your thinking that your head feels like it's spinning; or recognizing that you've temporarily turned into someone very different from your usual self.

3. Sleeping much more or much less than usual.

4. Picking fights with others or becoming supersensitive to what others say or do.

5. Feeling more anxious than usual.

6. Feeling increased sadness and depression.

As you look over this list, try to remember if there's anything else you do when you are upset by old memories.

Choosing the Right Vehicle for Traveling Down Memory Lane

Although distancers share basic styles of being in relationship and common bonds in the challenges of their childhoods, each person has to determine what will be the best process for remembering, analyzing, and absorbing her or his formative experiences of the past. There are a variety of processes you can utilize for remembering your childhood and getting to the core of the experiences that formed your adult distancing patterns. Some people use all the methods described below, while others concentrate most of their efforts using just one approach.

Contemplation and Assimilation

For some people, the most important part of remembering is to contemplate the various possibilities among the relevant childhood experiences that led to adult distancing, and then assimilate the new information. They may do this in one long, concentrated burst of thinking, journal writing, meditating, or grieving, or they may process their memories more gradually, letting in a little bit of new information at a time. People who favor this process tend to approach life as a series of puzzles to solve, using rational thinking to strengthen and change.

Rick's Story

Because he had been sexually abused, Rick had kept everything in his life tightly controlled. It was very important to him to feel that he was still in charge when it came to investigating his childhood and learning how it had shaped the roots of his distancing patterns. He discussed his memories without much emotion, then he began reading about the impact of sexual abuse and, gradually, arrived at an intellectual acceptance that the abuse had created lasting problems for him.

Once he felt that he was in control of the situation by absorbing all the information he could gather, he was slowly able to allow the emotional impact to surface. Bit by bit, he was able to assimilate both the cognitive and the emotional information about himself, and use it productively to understand and change his present-day relationships.

Investigation and Verification

People who need to approach their painful memories through some kind of activity instead of intellectual contemplation often prefer to use the process of investigation and verification. If this approach is your preference, you may want to get started right away. You can do this by talking to others who share the same family history, or were part of very similar families, to investigate and verify your memories.

This approach may also involve attending support groups and actively sharing similar memories of growing up in dysfunctional families. The families may have had abusive or alcoholic or drug-addicted parents or other relatives, or the children may have had to cope with a mentally ill parent, or struggle with geographical dislocation, or the many stresses of poverty. Regardless of the cause of the dysfunction, children growing up under these kinds of circumstances often suffer and cope in similar ways.

Reading groups can also work well for this style of processing: joining in a book group discussion about growing up with impaired or unhappily married parents may help to galvanize the process of investigation and verification.

Yvonne's Story

When Yvonne's book club read a memoir about childhood sexual abuse, she finally felt able to share her own history of sexual abuse with others. This freed her to share more of her history and herself with her boyfriend, validating for both of them that her complex responses to being sexual are very common among survivors of sexual abuse.

Creativity as a Healing Tool

People who best process emotionally charged information by using the nonverbal parts of their brains may prefer creative methods to explore their past and assimilate it into the present. Whether or not you think of yourself as creative, you may find that you feel more capable of absorbing your formative childhood experiences through the use of visual, tactile, and somatic experiencing. This might mean that you focus on experiencing where your memories are most powerfully felt in your body. For example, maybe when you think about your childhood, you get a heavy feeling in your gut. You could try drawing a picture of that feeling and then transform the heaviness into something lighter. Using this approach, you can experiment with transforming your memories into useful tools through your creative outlets.

Ben's Story

As Ben continued to learn more about why he had become such an entrenched distancer, he also added a new activity to his life that helped him in his exploration of his childhood. He began experimenting with carving wood, sometimes doing abstract carving, other times carving representations of faces that illuminated his emotional reconstruction of his past.

Janine's Story

Janine began to write poems about the strengths she was beginning to see in herself as she went through her painful process of remembering. She created powerful, transformative images in her poems: flowers that bloomed between the cracks of the cement sidewalks, thunderstorms that left glistening forests in their wake, and rocks that cracked wide open to reveal delicate veins.

Tools to Help You Learn from Your Memories

There are a variety of ways for you to continue working with Step Two. You'll find that no matter how you do your best learning and processing, it will be helpful to try out several different ways to do the work. Also, you'll need to find a variety of ways to take care of yourself throughout this process as you piece together your past and begin to understand how it shaped the person you are now. Here are some exercises you can use as tools or guidelines to continue the work you are now doing in Step Two.

Exercise
Somatic and Creative Work

Whether or not you are drawn to using creativity as a tool, the following exercise will help you experience using different parts of your brain to work with your memories.

Make sure you have at least thirty minutes of uninterrupted time to complete this exercise. Prepare yourself for it by getting some notebook or drawing paper and some colored pencils or markers. Try to find a quiet place where you can sit comfortably.

Part One: Follow the steps you've already learned to relax your body and slow down your breathing. Begin to allow yourself to picture some of those difficult situations you experienced in childhood. Tune in to your body as you sit here in the present moment, and see whether any part of your body feels strong sensations like pain, tension, or other discomfort. If you feel any of these sensations, try to picture how that body sensation would look if you drew a picture of it. Would it look like a burning fire? A huge, heavy pile of rocks? A giant ice cube? Stay with it for a few minutes.

Now, see if you can draw an image of that sensation, using colors and shapes to give yourself a rough idea of what you just discovered.

Part Two: Now go back into just relaxing your body and slowing down your breathing. When you are relaxed and breathing regularly, once again picture the childhood situations that caused you distress. Again, see where you feel the memories most strongly in your body. Again, see what sensations arise, what images, colors, and shapes these sensations might look like. Stay with these for a few minutes.

This time, try drawing some healing images. What could soothe a burning sensation? What could take the place of those heavy rocks? What would melt that giant ice cube?

Deconstructing the exercise: There are several purposes for doing this exercise. One is to help you use the nonverbal parts of your brain to investigate your memories, so that you can see what your body and the visualizing, sensing parts of your brain can teach you. Another purpose is to show you how to use other parts of your brain to get through the distress that the process of remembering may bring up. In part two of the exercise, you had the opportunity to transform a distressing memory so that you could go on to work more effectively with what you need to know about yourself.

Getting Yourself to the Starting Gate

You are about ready to begin authoring your autobiography; that is, connecting your memories of childhood with your current relationship challenges. Sometimes, it can be hard to get yourself into an energetic, active place to do the work of this nature. It's very easy to slip into a passive stance where you take in a lot of information, and then allow your emotions to take over. Or some people find they just want to run away from this experience, and they try to block difficult memories using any number of avoidance tactics.

However, the whole purpose of going back into the past is to use it as a tool. You'll feel much better once you start actively working with your tools. Here's another exercise to get you started.

Exercise

Sentence Completion

This exercise will help you focus on what's most significant in your store of memories, what it is that plays the biggest role in your current intimate connections. Remember to give yourself enough time to do this completely, and then let yourself write whatever first comes into your head. You can always go back later and add more details or rethink your answers; you can even change them. Now, complete the following sentences:

1. My parents' marriage made me think that ________________

   ____

   ____

2. As a child, my dream for when I grew up was that __________

   ____

   ____

   (If your answer is something like "become a fireman" or "live in a big city," see if you can add any wishes about love or marriage or children. If you can't, then that's something to think about too.)

3. Growing up, the most important thing I learned about love was

   ____

   ____

4. As a child, I was often afraid that ______________________

   ____

   ____

5. I was taught to value certain things about myself like ________

   ____

   ____

6. Sometimes I felt bad about myself because ______________________

____

____

7. Most people I knew during my childhood believed the most important thing about a spouse (partner) was ____________________

____

____

8. I learned to be careful what I said and to whom I said it because

____

____

9. I used to believe it was my fault that ____________________________

____

____

10. The biggest loss I remember from my childhood was ___________

____

____

11. The biggest disappointment I remember from my childhood was ____

____

12. The worst fear I had in childhood was ___________________________

____

____

13. I was often angry as a child because _____________________________

____

____

14. I knew that I didn't want to be like my mother (or father) when I grew up because ____

____

____

15. I wanted to be like my mother (or father) when I grew up because ____

____

____

16. To me, the ideal couple was ____________________ because

____

____

17. As a kid, I felt responsible for my mother (or father) when she (he) needed ____

____

____

18. I was proud of my family because ____________________

____

____

19. I was ashamed of my family because ____________________

____

____

20. I felt closest to ____________________ because he or she

____

____

If you found that you didn't feel clear about or were not interested in some of these statements you may find that you want to come back and try them again later. There are no special revelations that you should expect to have by analyzing your responses to these statements. This is just a way to get you to start working on what you need to remember and to record about the relevance of your childhood experience.

Writing Your Autobiography

Now it's time for you to get your journal and write a few pages about yourself and how various aspects of your childhood may have formed the most important roots of your distancing patterns. You don't need to write this as if you're writing an essay for publication. Just let yourself write, forgetting about spelling, grammar, and style. This is for your eyes only.

As you do this important exercise, you may find that you feel scattered, your thoughts going to one area of childhood experience and then veering off to something else. You may discover that something you hadn't thought much about becomes more important than you expected. You also may discover that you're writing what feels like a whole book on just one part of your childhood. It's all okay. Just remember that the purpose of writing your autobiography is to help you connect your childhood with what's going on in your life right now.

You can work on this in more than one writing session. In fact, when you first start it, you will want and need to take some breaks from the writing. You may need some more time just to think about what you're writing and to allow new thoughts to circle around in your mind before you come back to expand on or deepen what you began writing.

You may also find that bringing up painful thoughts and feelings is a pretty intense experience. This is normal. Take special care of yourself, though. Take a walk, take a bath, call a friend, play with the cat, take a break from your thoughts and read a mystery or watch a movie. While you are writing, always remember to use your breathing and muscle relaxation skills.

Sharing what you're discovering and feeling also may feel right to you. Make sure that you feel trust in the person or people you choose to confide in. If you are in therapy, you may want to spend some time talking this over with your therapist. If you are in a relationship, you may want to share this with your partner. If you have any hesitations, wait! When we get to Step Three, you will have the opportunity to do some work with your partner that includes sharing what you've been learning about yourself in Step Two. You will be guided to do careful sharing with your partner so that the experience will help the two of you become closer rather than leaving you feeling raw and exposed and leaving your partner wondering how to respond.

In chapter 4 we will continue working with Step Two by remembering and learning from past relationships in adult life. This will be a less intense and less time-consuming part of Step Two. We will look at lessons learned from past relationships, but avoid dwelling on what went wrong, what was wrong with the other person, or what you think were your mistakes. This chapter will help those who are not in relationships now, those who are in both new and long-term relationships, and those who have avoided relationships completely.

4 Step Two, Part Two: Learning from Past Relationships

This chapter will guide you through the second part of Step Two, which is to look at the past relationships in your adult life. Instead of trying to forget your past—the mistakes, the heartbreak, the regret for the one who got away—you will learn how to make good use of what went wrong in the past. We turn now to focus on these relationships because they are an essential part of your ongoing examination of the roots of your distancing patterns. Just as you learned in chapter 3, the first part of Step Two, your past is a resource; it contains a wealth of useful information and precious experience.

The Power of Past Adult Relationships

Just as in childhood, there are pivotal experiences in our adult lives that determine the pattern of our responses in subsequent relationships. Adult experiences may have somewhat less power over us because we've already developed our basic biological, emotional, and mental characteristics. Nonetheless, we are always changing and growing and we are deeply affected by our adult experiences in both positive and negative ways.

It's undeniable that if we experience trauma or tragic losses, that will have great importance in determining many things about who we are from that time on. For example, all those who have ever lost their homes because of a natural disaster, or social upheaval, or personal misfortune know that their feelings of personal safety and security will never be the same again. Other tragic events such as the loss of a child, a sibling, a close friend, or a life partner also change us permanently. But these tragic experiences can create new energy or spiritual awakening or a transformative life purpose, despite the awfulness of the loss.

Other major life events can create major changes in how we respond to the world. For example, someone may experience lasting repercussions from a life-threatening or life-altering accident or illness. Again, these kinds of experiences can create a new resilience that serves to counterbalance disability, fear, bitterness, and depression.

Addiction is another circumstance of adult life that creates its own set of responses in individuals and their loved ones. There is a broad spectrum of addictive behaviors that can change the course of an adult's life, including well-recognized addictions to substances like alcohol, drugs, and food, and the sometimes less obvious "process" addictions like gambling, overspending, self-injury, sex, work, computer activities, television, and exercise. If you've struggled with an addiction yourself or been involved with an addicted person, you are well aware that this fact of life determines a lot about how you respond in the area of intimate relationships.

Seemingly neutral life events such as changing jobs or getting promoted, buying a house, having a baby, moving from one geographical area to another, getting deeply involved in community activism, religious activities, sports, or hobbies can also make a big difference in how we respond to intimacy.

In most cases, however, past relationships probably trump any of the types of formative events mentioned above. For the majority of distancers, their past relationships continue to play a major role in their current lives. It sometimes seems as though we repeat the worst of our childhood nightmares in the relationships we create in early adult life. There are many variations among the relational experiences of people who struggle with distancing. It's likely that some of the themes and exercises that follow will resonate with you much more than others, depending on your personal history of intimate relationships.

Variables That Influence Relationships

There are some predictable variables in the overall history of your relationships that probably left their mark on you and even had an impact on those relationships you may not think of as significant in and of themselves. These variables can include:

- The sum total of distressing or failed relationships in the individual's life: that is, if you've had a lot of failed relationships, each one adds to the picture you may develop about yourself in relationship (for example, victim, heartbreaker, "not really interested," "too busy for love," and so forth).

- The length or emotional intensity of the most significant relationships: that is, the longer you are with someone, the more you are likely to be affected by the distress or failure of the relationship.

- Leaving relationships frequently: the more often you leave relationships, the more likely you are to develop a picture of yourself as a "quitter" or some other negative label that can make you defensive.

- Experiencing frequent betrayal or rejection.

- Exploring relationships but avoiding commitment.

- Avoiding intimate relationships consistently.

Because of all these variables and more, there may be some issues that seem a good fit with your life experiences while other issues won't resonate for you. As you answer some of the questions in this chapter and compare yourself with other distancers' relational histories in the following thumbnail sketches, you'll notice which are the most important for you.

Also, there are other factors that may play a role in how much you can identify with other people's stories about their past relationships. These identifying factors include your age, your gender, your relational orientation (heterosexual, gay, lesbian, bisexual, celibate), your religious affiliation, your social and economic background and current options, your involvement with extended family, and other socioeconomic factors.

Although any or all of these may have been important in how you experienced your past relationships, there is no guarantee that because someone is similar to you in these categories you will have had the same experiences in couple relationships. Conversely, you may be surprised at how much you identify with someone who, on the surface, appears to be very different from you. For example, you may have a strong connection with your extended family, but this doesn't necessarily mean that you will respond to intimate relationships just like someone else who has the same kind of strong family ties.

Now, let's take a look at two distancers you've already read about, Sally and Luisa. Sally comes from a closely connected family like Luisa's, but her way of distancing from a committed relationship is different than Luisa's. Sally stays in relationship, and she makes few demands on her partner, Howard, but she remains elusive; she's too busy and distracted to engage in intimacy. Luisa, on the other hand, distances by attacking; she arms herself with rigid judgments about her partner, Diego.

Although both women began shaping their distancing patterns in childhood, and went on to amplify those patterns in their unhappy adult relationships, their similarities are less significant than their differences.

It is vital to understand how your past relationships shaped how you respond in the present. If you don't understand this, you may go on to experience a series of disappointments that can lead only to deeper despair and greater self-blame. But looking at your past is not easy. Here's how you can get yourself through this part of Step Two without feeling worse or giving up.

Observing with Detachment

You can use the issues and exercises in this chapter as a map to help you explore and touch down briefly on a few of the most important legacies of your past relationships. You won't need to review and revisit every intimate relationship you've ever had or ever wanted to have. We're working with this part of Step Two just to highlight a few of the past experiences that changed you significantly and provided you with lessons about yourself in intimate situations.

Unlike experiences you may have had when talking to a friend, therapist, or new love interest, this review of your past relationships is not about your ex-partner (or partners). Although there were undoubtedly many negative and positive things about those people, understanding them is not central to the work of Step Two. The process of remembering in Step Two is all about who you are and what you've learned about yourself from your past experiences as an adult.

How Past Relationships Leave Their Mark

It can sometimes seem as if we are doomed to repeat the worst experiences of our childhood in our adult relationships. This can leave us completely confused, wondering if we are once again the victim of neglect, abuse, or whether we've become the victimizer when we unintentionally harm those we love.

Victim or Victimizer

There are many different ways that past relationships can leave their mark on you. The repetition of being the one who feels repeatedly rejected in relationships may create a self-image of "victim" that clouded the underlying distancing issues you've carried with you into each relationship. Jack's series of relationships provide a very typical scenario.

Jack's Story

Jack's many relationships with women were like a parody of an old Mother Goose nursery rhyme. He was always jumping over the relational candlestick, trying to avoid being burned, without much success. There seemed to be an endless succession of women who alternately loved him and left him. Several of Jack's partners, like Diane, became frequent flyers.

With each successive relationship failure, Jack became less self-confident. Although he appeared to want a lasting relationship, he grew ever more proficient at finding partners who would outdistance him. His relationship with Diane was the most extreme in terms of the number of their breakups. But Diane wasn't the first woman to dance the "make up and break up tango" with Jack, and she would not be the last. For Jack, each successive relationship created a deeper wound and an ever-increasing tendency to repeat his distancing patterns.

Having the experience of failed relationships can create the distancer pattern of running away from healthy relationships, too. Sally's story represents this kind of escalation.

Sally's Story

Sally grew more and more self-blaming when she first began to watch herself distancing from Howard. She had fled from her first marriage to escape the burden of being forced to be a mother to her husband. Her leaving reinforced her growing image of herself as hard-hearted and unfair. But she had not adequately resolved her decision to leave her first marriage, so her self-blame became almost immobilizing as she felt herself pulling away from Howard.

When the Painful Past Builds Higher Walls

The fear of beginning a new relationship can become greatly intensified by failed relational attempts. Some distancers react to failed relationships by becoming more extreme in their avoidance patterns. Others use the experience of being wounded to sharpen their weapons against subsequent partners or would-be partners.

Janine's Story

Janine had been emotionally scarred by her early adult experience of gang rape. When she tried to date, she was so afraid of seeming vulnerable that she hid behind an impenetrable wall of evasive communication and disappearing behavior. One young man did manage to get a bit closer than anyone else, partly due to his own ambivalent relational style. When Janine began to allow herself to risk a relationship with him, he suddenly disappeared, which left her feeling even more vulnerable and mistrustful.

Colin's Story

Colin had been deeply harmed not only by his mother's rejection of him as a child, but when he was a young man, he had his heart broken by the woman he thought was his "true love." Colin had found the woman he believed was the love of his life at the age of twenty-five. They met when he was finishing law school, and they began a joyous and passionate relationship that promised to heal all of his childhood wounds. He began to think he was going to have it all: a brilliant career defending the rights of the oppressed, and a fairy-tale marriage that would carry him into the sunset and last until the end of his life.

Unfortunately, Colin's alcoholic drinking continued to create huge problems for the otherwise happy young couple. Colin's girlfriend had not grown up as he had in an alcoholic family; she found his drinking extremely confusing and disturbing. Finally, she gave him the ultimatum that if he didn't stop drinking, she would have to leave him. Colin rejected Alcoholics Anonymous for dealing with his alcoholism, and, despite a brief effort at abstinence, he remained an active alcoholic. When the love of his life became the one who got away, Colin blamed her and all the subsequent women he met later in life for whatever went wrong with his relationships.

When Rigid Rules Hold You Back

Failures to communicate successfully in past relationships can cause people to set up rigid rules for their new relational efforts. This can happen when someone feels inadequate, attacked, or betrayed in an earlier relationship.

Chris's Story

Chris might have been a little more open to the positive benefits of directly expressing her feelings had it not been for her past relationship with Molly. Chris and Molly's relationship had lasted for two years, and almost kept Chris from ever finding Beth.

Chris got involved with Molly soon after graduating from college. Molly, a lovely young woman who lived in the same apartment building, was embroiled in a custody battle to keep her young daughter. Chris tried to help her. Molly's ex-husband claimed that because of her sexual orientation, Molly was an unfit mother. Chris and a group of her friends championed Molly's right to her child, and supported her in every way they could. When the dust settled, Molly had her daughter. Chris continued trying to make life better for Molly and her child. Then Chris and Molly got romantically involved, and Chris invited mother and child to move in with her.

Things went steadily downhill from there. Molly had a huge appetite for "processing" all of her emotional wounds. She had commandeered hours of Chris's time whenever she felt upset by something Chris said or did, or didn't say or do. Molly was also prone to sudden rage attacks, and she had asserted her need to fully "vent her anger to avoid the physical aches and pains caused by repressed feelings." After she finally moved out of Chris's life, Chris swore she would never get into a relationship again.

Sexual Obstacles

Sex can be both wonderful and complicated even under the best of conditions. When sexual problems arise in adult relationships, they often worsen because, for most people, it's difficult to talk about what's bothering or confusing them. Frequently, both people in the relationship develop the belief that only one of them is to blame for whatever isn't going well. This can escalate into blaming all past partners, potential partners, or all men (or women).

Rick's Story

For Rick, who had never been able to talk about the sexual abuse he suffered as a child, it felt impossible to talk with his wife Carla about his extreme need for sexual control. He disliked it when she took the initiative to get things going sexually, and any attempt on her part to change their routine sexual patterns was intolerable to him.

Rick had become engaged to Carla just before he left home for his military service, but he got into a relationship with a servicewoman he met while he was serving in the Middle East. Since this was a secret relationship, this experience only intensified his childhood feelings of guilt and shame about sex. Both Rick and his new partner had someone waiting for them at home, so they agreed to limit their affair just to the time they were stationed abroad. By repeating the abuse dynamics from his childhood, Rick was engaged in a secret sexual relationship that he believed was wrong.

Yvonne's Story

When Yvonne became a teenager and was no longer subjected to sexual abuse, she was not sexual with anyone. This changed when she was in her early twenties. She had a brief affair with her boss, a man who was significantly older than she. Yvonne enjoyed his attentions, and she felt sexually powerful when she was with him because he was always so grateful for her sexual favors. He ended the relationship after asking her to marry him and being rejected.

Yvonne carried her guilt and discomfort from this relationship into each subsequent one, and the experience continued to cast a shadow over her efforts to be open and loving with any man, including her current boyfriend.

Idealizing Past Relationships

Some people use an idealized past relationship to keep all the possible later partners at a distance. This is often the case when one distancer finds another, and experiences the distancing maneuvers as both safe and tantalizing. Both during and after the relationship both distancers may idealize everything about the ex-lover and the relationship without recognizing that what they are idealizing is the perfect mirror image.

Ben's Story

Ben had allowed himself to stay in a long-term relationship only once. He had gotten into a much more settled relationship with Liz than anyone before or since. He thought of his long-past relationship with Liz as the gold standard against which all other relationships failed to measure up. Liz had always been very busy, a community activist who advocated for the rights of animals, children, mental patients, and many other disenfranchised groups.

Ben appreciated his partner's passions and commitments, but he often found himself wishing that she were more available to spend time with him. This tinge of loneliness felt very strange to him because he greatly valued his freedom after having escaped his mother's suffocating preoccupation with him. On the other hand, he felt a pleasant edge of desire for Liz that never disappeared since she was always so elusive. Even when they lived together, Liz outdistanced Ben. She was either off on one of her missions or filling the house with people who were part of her many social activist organizations.

Liz went to such extremes of unavailability that eventually Ben left her, but he was miserable in the wake of the failed relationship. Although they eventually became good friends, he never stopped believing that she had been the love of his life. No one else could dance away from him in the same endlessly desirable swirl of activity. He also convinced himself that he had been the victim in the relationship, so that he wasn't always the heartbreaker.

As you can see from reading these various examples about the effects of past relationships on the formation of distancing patterns, there are a number of ways that distancers can experience and process their past adult relationships. It would be an impossible task to categorize all the possibilities, so if you haven't found your experience described here, that doesn't mean that you are somewhere off the grid.

Now, you can begin working on your own story, searching through your old memories for the moments that led you to this point in time.

Reconstructing Your Relational Landmarks

To help you get started looking at your past relationships, here's a warm-up exercise that will help you go back in time to remember what may have been an influential past relationship.

Exercise
"First Love"

Pick up your journal, open to a blank page, and write a few paragraphs about your first love affair or first couple relationship. Don't spend a lot of time thinking about it. Describe what thrilled you about the person. Describe how the other people in your life responded to this relationship. For example, how did your friends, family, religious or neighborhood community feel about you being with this person?

Next, name a few things this person valued most about being in a relationship with you. What about you? Did you value the same things? What do you remember as the most challenging part about this first experience? How did it end? How did you feel about its ending?

If you had to choose a title for your first experience of being in (or wanting to be in) a couple relationship, what would the title be? Examples might be: "Young and Innocent," or "Love Hurts," or "Me and My Shadow," or "What Was I Thinking?"

Deconstructing the exercise: This exercise has several functions. It's designed to get you to focus on the task of extracting useful information from your past. It will also provide you with some clues about what you used to believe about love and whether your beliefs have changed since then. You may learn that how you feel about your first love has played an important role ever since in how you respond to or think about relationships.

Note: You may decide that the relationship you've just recalled took place when you were so young that it didn't really make a significant groove in your relational memory. If so, you might want to do the exercise again, but this time use a later relationship to see if you can learn more. On the other hand, you may decide that your early experience definitely had a significant bearing on who you are today.

Lessons Learned from Past Relationships

As you can see, there are many ways to reconstruct the past. It doesn't matter much what you remember about the specific details of a past partner's emotional or relational profile. It doesn't really matter what did or didn't happen in terms of significant events, or who said and did what during a major argument. It doesn't even really matter why the relationships ended. What you are trying to discover is what you learned from your past efforts in intimate relationships. What lessons did you take with you when the relationship ended? You are looking for clues about what might have shaped your current ideas, fears, dreams, tender places, and sore spots.

So, instead of getting lost in your happy and unhappy memories on this trip down Memory Lane, you should look for the signposts that signal what your past relationships have to teach you. You want to discern what stands out as important danger warnings and what the welcome signs were, too. You are looking back for the relationships that taught your gut to flash "Danger, Falling Rocks!" so that you learned to keep your eyes open. You are also looking for what you learned about your ability to find the bypass signs that allow you to detour past the worst of the swamps and sinkholes.

Use the following exercise to remind yourself about some of the things your past relational history has taught you about yourself.

Exercise

What Do You Know About Yourself?

Check off any of the following statements that are a good fit for you. Put an asterisk next to those that seem to fit particularly well.

1. I'm afraid of being consumed by a partner's needs, desires, and opinions. ______
2. I'm afraid of being rejected by potential (or current) partners. ______
3. I'm afraid a partner will leave me. ______

4. I'm not good at setting limits. (I'm either too vague or too rigid.) ______

5. I don't make compromises easily. ______

6. I'm afraid of being inadequate (not interesting enough, or not generous enough, or not loving enough). ______

7. I have a lot of sexual anxiety. (For example, I don't know how to ask for what I want. I keep my real sexual responses concealed. I space out during sex. I fantasize about being with another person during sex.) ______

8. I need more time alone (or quiet time) than a lot of other people do. ______

9. I don't need as much time alone with a partner as other people seem to need. (I like to be with other friends, family, with or without my partner.) ______

10. I don't know how to get the validations I need from a partner. ______

11. I get bored easily as soon as I start to get settled into a relationship. ______

12. I often compare myself to my partners (or potential partners) and feel shame, jealousy, or self-contempt. ______

13. I tend to be very critical of partners or potential partners. ______

14. I do much better in couple relationships with partners who share my values and interests. ______

15. I find it much easier to give than to receive. ______

16. I've learned that honesty doesn't really always pay. ______

17. I don't want my partner to tell me what's wrong with me or how I should do things. ______

18. I feel that I'm too demanding to be in a relationship. ______

19. I don't trust people easily, especially those who tell me they are attracted to me or like me. ______

20. I think I'm a real "catch" because I've learned so much from my past relationships. ______

In your journal, you can add anything else to this list that you think might be an important aspect of who you are in relationships. You've learned both positive and potentially difficult things about yourself when you are in a relationship, so allow yourself to think about both the "good" and the "bad" as you add to your list.

When you've finished adding to the list, go back to the items you noted as being especially true for you. Take a few minutes to reflect on which of these items seem most relevant to certain past relationships of yours. Start by writing the partner's name who helped you to recognize this about yourself. (You may find there are several names attached to some or all of these items.) Keep this fact in mind: the best teachers may be the people with whom you had the most difficult relationships.

If you are having trouble matching the most important items with specific people, don't worry about it right now. You are engaged in a process of remembering that tends to stir up all kinds of memory fragments and random associations. Just keep on writing down whatever connections come to you. It's all useful.

Whether or not you were able to match specific names to the self-awareness items in the above list, you may want to make a few notes about those you highlighted as most important. You could note whether this lesson you've learned about yourself is something you'd like to change or not. You could note whether what you feel most strongly about is an old awareness or a new one. You could note whether or not your ex-partners would agree or disagree with any of your self-awareness lessons. You could note if some of these items have changed over time.

If you feel that this is a useful exercise and you want to go into more detail, go ahead and write further about any of the lessons you've learned and which were the relationships that taught you the most. Or if you feel that this is enough for now, you can end the exercise, knowing that you can always come back to do more work with this later on, after you've had time to reflect.

Remembering Your Strengths

As you do this work, it's also important to look back on the strengths that you learned you had. For each unsuccessful or incomplete relationship in your past, there are also moments for you to honor. For example, you had the strength to leave, or to survive the ending of relationships that might once have promised everything. You learned more about yourself from each missed connection or bruised feeling or wounded heart. You can look back on the relationships, or "almost" relationships, or fantasies of relationship, and see them as valuable building blocks in your creation of a whole self.

These past relationships (including those that didn't really ever take off) are like books in a library that you've created, stories you've written, read, or collected about your journey through a vital part of human experience. You own the complete, collected works of you. You are the author and you can go back to check out all the separate parts of your story whenever you need to.

Exercise

Healing Exercise

Reviewing old relationships is hard work emotionally, no matter how carefully you've been trying to use your past as material to study in the service of creating a healthier present. This is a great opportunity to practice some self-care work to heal any old wounds that you may have opened doing the last exercise. Take about twenty minutes or so to do this next exercise. It will help you soothe any distress you may be feeling.

First, get into a comfortable sitting position so you can feel relaxed without falling asleep. If you enjoy listening to soothing music or ambient sounds, such as ocean waves, you may want to use that as background. Make sure you won't be interrupted by people or phones ringing or any other predictable distractions.

Also, you might want to tape-record this visualization exercise for yourself or get someone to read it to you. That way, you can relax completely and let yourself be in the experience, rather than trying to remember what you are supposed to be doing.

Instructions: Close your eyes (or just look at one place on the floor if closing your eyes makes you feel too spaced out or sleepy) and take some slow, deep breaths, paying attention only to the sensation of your breathing. Now begin to slow down your breathing. Remind your muscles to relax and let go of any tension.

Imagine that you're in a favorite peaceful place. Picture the surroundings, feel the air against your skin, listen to any sounds that you usually enjoy hearing in this favorite place. As you continue to picture this place, invite someone comforting to come into that place with you. (You may prefer the company of an animal or a presence; for example, invite your Higher Power, or Spirit, instead of a person.) Just enjoy the picture in your mind of being in that favorite place with this comforting person or presence.

Picture yourself handing over your past disappointments, hurts, and losses to this person or presence. Ask this being to take away these burdens from you, trusting that you can say good-bye to old memories of suffering without having to forget the people attached to the memories.

When this being has taken away your burdens, give yourself a little time to continue picturing yourself in this favorite place. Give yourself permission to feel lighter and freer. When you are ready, you can slowly return to the present moment, letting yourself know that you can always go back to this place to meet this special being again, whenever you need to hand over your old memories of suffering and lighten your emotional load.

If you have trouble allowing yourself to do this kind of exercise with a whole heart, you can always experiment with giving yourself a simple reminder to relax and let go of past memories of suffering.

Using the Past to Build a Stronger Future

We will end the work of Step Two by consolidating what you've learned from your past relationships into solid building blocks for the foundation of your future relationship enterprise. You've now worked with what the past has taught you, and this is useful information to guide you into the future.

We'll start by making a red-flag list of the people you've learned you must avoid.

Exercise

Red-Flag List

Everyone has a different set of danger signals that they learn to watch for, whether they're hoping to begin a new relationship or wondering if they should leave their current partner. Here's a typical "red flag" list:

People to stay away from:

- People who don't seem curious about who I am
- People who seem to be overloaded with problems and needs
- People who never seem to stay in relationships for long
- People who don't have much going on in their lives
- People who always have too much going on in their lives
- People who don't share my fundamental values
- People who don't enjoy activities like ________________ (fill in the blank with what really matters a lot to you, for example, outdoor activities, or cultural events, just hanging out at home, or doing social stuff with groups of friends and/or extended family)
- People who don't like ________________ (fill in the blank with categories like children, or animals, or whatever really matters to you)
- People who are too opinionated (or those who have no passionate convictions about anything)

- People who always need to be in control of everything
- People who seem constantly angry, depressed, or anxious
- People who always get jealous of what I have (for example, my job, my income, my skills, my friends)

When you've finished looking over these examples, write down your own red-flag list. You may notice that it resembles what you've been reviewing about what you learned from past relationships. Notice whether there are any surprises. You might decide that you want to avoid people who don't like animals for example, not so much because you have pets but because of what you've learned about people in the past who didn't like animals. Maybe the ex-partner who was the most jealous of everything you had didn't like animals. You've learned that you must stay away from these types of people because they won't allow you to really enjoy whatever you have and love, including pets or the possibility of pets.

Now, you are finally at the brink of stepping into the world of making a new relational life for yourself. You've used your awareness skills to focus on who you've been in past relationships, and you've journeyed through memories of your childhood and previous adult life. Now, you have enough self-knowledge to consciously design the kind of relational future you deserve.

Exercise
Your Wish List

You can use your self-knowledge to design your ideal relationship. Throw away all the abbreviated descriptions from the Personals section of the newspaper, or the mindless requests for the perfect partner in the outer reaches of cyberspace. Here's your chance to create a wish list based on what you've come to know about yourself in relationships.

The following examples will help you develop your own specifications for a healthy relationship. You can use this as a checklist, and once again use an asterisk to indicate an especially important item:

In my ideal relationship…

I'm looking for stability, and safety, and a reasonable amount of predictability. ______

I'm looking for someone who will be committed and faithful. ______

I'm looking for a relationship with flexibility and plenty of "breathing room." ______

I'm looking for someone who affirms and supports who I am and what I do. ______

I'm looking for someone who gets me out of my head and out into life. ______

I'm looking for someone who's a good friend and companion. ______

I'm looking for someone who doesn't overwhelm me with his or her needs. ______

I'm looking for more romance and excitement. ______

I'm looking for someone who understands me, someone who "gets" who I am. ______

I'm looking for someone who's similar to me (or is part of my world). ______

Use this list to get started making your own list. You can make the longest list you want to. Don't edit yourself by being too reasonable. Let yourself write down whatever you think you really want in a relationship. Also, let yourself be as specific as you want to be; for example, "I want someone who has always dreamed of going to the Grand Canyon to watch the sun rise," or "I want a partner who is good at fixing things around the house," or "I want a partner who can help me to learn to tango and look good doing it."

____

Exercise
Writing Your Dream Story

To conclude Step Two, take as much time as you need to write a short story about your ideal relationship. (This exercise applies to you even if you're currently in a relationship. Just imagine that in your short story, the couple is transformed into your ideal relationship.)

Before you begin to write your short story, here are a few things to think about. You don't have to share this story with anyone. It's for your eyes only. Just relax and write. This exercise will help you to envision all of what matters the most to you in a relationship. It will also help you to make your vision become reality. The more thoughtfully we picture our goals, the more likely we are to get what we want.

Write about the things you and your partner appreciate about each other. Describe what you do together day by day. Create a few special events or moments that you share (this could even be facing something difficult together). Write about how you work together to make a good life, including the challenges that face any couple when the going gets tough. Describe how you and your partner play together. Describe what makes you happy about this relationship. Write about how other people in your life respond to you as a couple. Write about the dreams you share with your partner in this ideal relationship.

You are putting together all the knowledge you've been gathering about yourself and your past. You are also beginning the work of transformation.

In the next two chapters you will work on how to make this ideal relationship happen as you practice making new connections between yourself and others, including your communities of support, and you'll learn how to create new connections with a partner. You will be able to do this because you have completed the work of building a very strong and deep foundation for your new life.

5 Step Three, Part One: Community—Where Transformation Begins

When you fully engage in community, your capacity for intimate relationships will automatically begin to change and improve.

Once again, the Awareness, Remembering, and Connecting (ARC) model challenges you to try a new approach to changing your relationships with others. You are about to begin a unique action plan for changing your basic approach to intimacy. You'll experience something different from any other approach to love and intimacy that you might have tried because rather than start with the couple relationship, we will begin with relationships you will build between yourself and your community.

As we move into the work of Step Three, you will experience how the transformation of your relational approach in groups can transform your relational capabilities at every level. Eventually, we will focus on intimate relationships, but not until you've first explored new ways to relate within group or community contexts. This chapter will help you understand and activate this secret to success in intimate relationships.

Why Change Begins in Community

Although it might seem more logical to focus on changes in your one-to-one relationships, you are about to discover why starting with groups is more likely to make changing your one-to-one relationships successful. Here are the primary reasons why you need to first deepen and expand your relationships within a group or community:

- When you get involved in a community or group, it *defuses* your fears and expectations about intimate relationships. That is, it decreases your anxieties, fears, and expectations around trying to create a perfect couple relationship.

  When you put all your energy into trying to get what you need from a couple relationship, often working twice as hard to protect yourself from vulnerability, you can easily get stuck in your old patterns of approach-avoidance, which are triggered by fear of failure. When you are engaged in satisfying relationships in the community or group of your choice, this intense pressure decreases.

- Give yourself a break. You can safely try out new ways of relating to others in a group or community context. Don't risk trying out your new ways of relating in the most problematic relationship of all, the couple. For example, suppose you fear being consumed in an intimate relationship. Your usual pattern might be to erect aggressive and impenetrable walls when a simple two-way conversation would be enough. So, your assignment for changing your distancing style is to practice setting less rigid boundaries. It will be much easier to experiment with this process in a group instead of doing it as one of a couple where your deepest vulnerability is at stake.

Here's another example. Suppose you're so afraid of closeness that in your quest for intimacy you always pursue people who are clearly unavailable. When you do the work of Step Three, you will make connections with members of a group who are more relationally available. This will increase your self-esteem and will give you the positive experience of making closer connections with available people.

- By fully engaging in almost any form of group or community, you will have more people to learn from, people whose actions and ways of being can teach you a lot about relationships. This can be particularly helpful when you have been stuck in a narrow, little emotional room filled with your solitary thoughts about closeness, or when you've been limiting yourself to the thoughts and beliefs contained within your couple relationship.

Beginning Step Three: Lights, Camera, ACTION!

Suppose you're feeling put off by the idea of getting yourself involved in community interactions, even if theoretically it makes sense to you. You can think about it this way: When you take the focus off your love life and meet your emotional needs in a different kind of social situation, it might allow you to relax and enjoy life a little more, right? So ... just let go and see what happens.

"But I don't do groups!" the average distancer may exclaim in horror. I know, I know. I was once right there with you, kicking and protesting against any suggestion of group activities or joining any form of community. "I like one-on-one relationships. That's it!" I replied when invited to participate in group activities. This was obviously not true or else I would have been happily nestled into a successful couple relationship! However, I was oblivious to my faulty logic.

For many reasons, groups or community might seem like the last thing any distancer would choose. Entering any form of community or group can feel strange, scary, even impossible. Nonetheless, if you take this leap of faith, weird as it may feel, you will discover that it is the most effective way to leave loneliness behind.

Tackling Your Resistance

What have you got to lose? You're already in the process of reevaluating your world, your operating modes, your whole identity, so you might as well keep on going. You are ready for change. If you weren't, you would accept your loneliness or unhappiness, and ignore the idea that maybe your relational life could feel a lot better. If you weren't ready to try to change your life, you might be curled up with the latest book by your favorite mystery writer, letting the world of relationships carry on without your presence. Instead of working with the exercises in *Stop Running from Love,* you could be reading a book about raising Yorkshire Terriers or making better investments.

Now you're ready to get started on the actual transactions that will transform your relationship patterns. You will be guided through a menu of opportunities for working on new relationships within a community. You'll concentrate on several areas of common relational challenge for distancers. But first you need more information about the concept of "community."

Defining "Community"

Let's start with a description of what we mean by "community." Stop worrying that you'll be told to join a group or cult you wouldn't wish on even your worst enemy. You won't have to go to community potlucks at the local neighborhood center or join a book club or sign up with the Welcome Wagon committee, although, if you did, you might find out that you enjoy such activities. You don't have to stop your already busy life and make space for a group or community affiliation that would eat up all your free time. You will explore only those groups or communities that fit your individual personality, interests, preferences, or beliefs. And you can participate as little or as much as you want.

Guess what? You're already a part of a community, whether you define it that way or not. That's because there are so many forms of community that each of us connects to in some way. You're already involved in various forms of community. So, first think about any group of people with whom you already have some affiliation.

You are very likely to be a member of a family. You are a resident of a town, city, or neighborhood. You are also likely to be part of a workplace community or job-based network of some sort. You may be affiliated with a spiritually based group, a recreational group, or a group that exists because of a shared interest in nature, hobbies, books, sports, community improvement, social change, music, and so forth. You may be involved in a support group, like a 12-step program, or an exercise or health-focused group. You may be part of the cyber community, participating in listservs, blogs, or chat rooms.

Exercise

Create Your Community Map

Begin by examining how you see yourself in relation to all the various forms of community that are already in your life. This exercise will help you picture how all these communities connect to you, both those from your past and those in your current life.

Instructions: Get a blank piece of paper and draw yourself as a face or stick figure in the center. Now, using a word or two to describe the various communities or groups in your life, jot these down, using as much of the space on the paper as you need. You can make the map easier to read by circling each word and drawing a line between it and your image in the center.

If you want to organize this exercise a little more, you can also try placing the groups that are currently most important in your life closer to your image. Or you can place past groups and communities on one side of the page, and current ones on the other side, creating a visual time line. Here's an example:

Young Adult Groups/Communities:
music groups (chorus, rock band, fan club)
women's consciousness-raising groups
work groups (researchers, daycare workers, carpenters)
family of origin
political action groups
friends

Early Midlife Years:
graduate school friends
work colleagues (therapists, supervisees, mentors)
students
family (adopted sisters, nieces, partners)

Current Groups/Communities:
Raging Grannies singing group
12-step support groups
tennis teams
current family (partner, stepdaughter, son-in-law, grandsons)
friends

Although the degree of your involvement may be a minor part of your daily life, your map illustrates that you already have the experience of being a part of various groups or communities. You also know that you have a variety of relationships with the other members of those groups.

You'll begin Step Three by focusing on how you connect with others in the communities you're already a part of, along with exploring new groups or communities that you may want to choose as your new frontier for exploring relational change.

Family: The Original Community

Let's start with the most likely common denominator for all of us, the family. You may be part of a close-knit family or you may feel detached or separated from your relatives, but you are part of a family in some way. We all start out in a family, and no matter the size or health of the family system, we form the core of our relational patterns based on what we experience in that original group, our first community.

Even if you have chosen to separate from the family you grew up in, or you've severed relationships with the family you created in adult life, you are never really without family. Family relationships live on in your memory, as do certain connections you make with others, including your pets, your friends, your dates, and your partners. They all produce familiar dynamics that relate to your family relationships. The original family continues to influence us in all the other communities we enter throughout our lives.

Sally's Story

For some of us, the word "family" can evoke warm feelings; for others, it brings up misery or revulsion. For Sally, who grew up in a large chaotic family with too many responsibilities, changing her relationships within her family of origin was a good place to begin working toward a different way of relating to others. Remember, her distancing pattern was to keep her husband at arm's length by always being too busy with their kids, her work, her friends, and the boundless support she provided for her siblings whenever they were in crisis.

Sally began by first recognizing and accepting herself as a typical distracted distancer, and then by examining the overfunctioning role she had played in her family of origin. She began her Step Three work by changing her role with all of her siblings. When either her brother or her middle sister went into one of their predictable crisis scenarios, Sally coached them to turn to each other for support instead of always turning to her. She also worked with her youngest sister and persuaded her to take responsibility for the family gatherings at holidays and birthdays. After some time, Sally was finally able to turn some of the family crisis-response tasks over to this previously disengaged sister.

Sally's biggest change in her relationships with her siblings came when she had to ask them all for help when she found herself in financial distress after Howard's back injury forced him to stop working.

The end result of Sally's changing role with her siblings was that she became able to ask her husband for more emotional support and she turned more of their family's responsibilities over to him. She stopped seeing him as yet one more potentially needy person. She could let herself become more open and available to him, as you will see in chapter 6.

Workplace Communities

Another common form of community for most of us is the workplace. Workplace communities can vary greatly in size and degree of intimacy, but they generally function to help us relate to others in a variety of group settings. Even those who are self-employed must engage in a set of work relationships that provide a form of community. A self-employed carpenter may spend many hours working alone, but he or she interacts with customers, material suppliers, contractors, and other tradespeople. A stay-at-home mother is necessarily based in her home, but this too is a workplace community comprised of her children, partner, friends, neighbors, school personnel, doctors, and everyone else she interacts with in her daily life.

If we spend a lot of our time working—and most of us do—workplace communities play a major role in our lives. Like the family, the workplace is also a community in which the relationships are not necessarily with people you would naturally choose as friends. This makes the workplace a great community to practice relational skills to learn how to "hang in there" with inescapable situations, such as having to share an office with people you don't really like, or working on a job with other workers who don't do things the way you think they should be done.

Jack's Story

Jack was prone to approach-avoidance relationships in his workplace, just as he was in his intimate relationships with the unavailable women he pursued. He was an instructor in the art department of a large university and was frequently pursued by his female students. He enjoyed his students' attentions and danced a thin line between graciousness and flirtation. Several of his faculty colleagues (female) tried hard to get Jack's attention, but he avoided their overtures because, although he didn't understand this at the time, they were too available.

Things changed for Jack after he began the work of recognizing his distancing patterns and tracing their roots back to the dynamics of his unhappy childhood. He slowly came to realize that his job was an unhealthy community for him because he was surrounded by unavailable women—his students—whose flirtations kept him stuck in a subtle form of the same approach-avoidance dance he had played out with Diane and the other distancers he had pursued. He realized he needed to find a community that would provide healthier work-based relationships.

Making a real commitment to the change-making work of Step Three, Jack decided to leave the safety of his university job. He began to produce and sell his artwork more regularly. He also began studying creative mediums he had never explored before. In the next chapter, you will learn how this led Jack to a lively, mutual relationship that developed through his new work network.

Vision-Based Communities

There are communities that draw people together because of a shared belief system or vision of making things better. For some people, getting involved in a church, temple, mosque, or meditation community may offer a comfortable way to get more involved with community relationships. For others, a shared conviction about social justice issues (peace, racial equality, neighborhood safety, environmental issues) may provide a way to expand and deepen nonintimate relationships.

Within such communities, there is often a solid base of shared values that support any disagreements and conflicts that occur between group members. For distancers who are afraid of confronting difficult or demanding issues within an intimate relationship, this kind of community can provide an ideal safety zone to explore how relationships can survive conflicts.

Chris's Story

Chris, who was so afraid that she and Beth couldn't survive a single argument, learned to stop fearing conflict after she got involved in a group that worked to support gays and lesbians' right to marriage. She observed people disagreeing with each other, sometimes quite heatedly, and yet after their arguments were resolved, they remained good-natured and friendly as they continued working together toward their common goal.

The turning point for Chris came when she got into an intense argument with a man in the group. She had been feeling very comfortable with Michael until they began arguing. She stopped suddenly in the middle of a sentence as she felt herself starting to freeze. She was sure he hated her, and that the whole group saw her as a troublemaker. "Sorry. I'm coming on too strong," she mumbled to Michael and the rest of the group. She began putting on her jacket so she could beat a hasty retreat out the door. She was sure she would never come back to the group.

"Hey, honey," Michael said, "don't back down on me now! We were just warming up. I've got four older sisters. It would take a whole lot more than what you just said for me to feel you were coming on too strong."

This was an important moment for Chris when she realized that within the group, conflict was not something to be avoided, and when it occurred, it didn't destroy relationships. After that, she began taking increasing risks, showing her feelings more spontaneously and learning that the other people in the group stayed connected to her whether she agreed with them or not.

Support Groups

Perhaps the most perfect community to help the distancer practice new relational skills is the traditional support group. For some, involvement in a support group is a lifelong commitment, while for others it may be time-limited. Whether the group has a permanent structure or is more temporary, a support group is generally a very safe place to practice relational risk-taking.

There are many kinds of support groups, but they are all based on the same principles. Everyone in the group needs support and everyone is there to give support as well as to receive it. The group shares a common experience that motivates them to seek help, information, acceptance, and hope. In a support group, everyone is equal because of their shared experiences of challenge, hardship, and their need to change. Everyone hopes to find a way out of individual suffering by participation in the group.

The support group is an ideal community for distancers because it demands some amount of vulnerability, some degree of accountability to the other group members (like showing up and following the guidelines for the group process). The average community of support permits a cautious pace and offers clearly defined boundaries that help the distancer to feel safe.

Colin's Story

Colin, the attorney whose sarcastic and judgmental behavior had caused him to be consistently rejected by the women in his life, found an ideal place to begin to work on relationships. After yet another initially dazzling romance ended badly, he finally faced his alcoholism and began attending meetings of Alcoholics Anonymous.

At first, he was contemptuous, making fun of the slogans and routines of the program whenever he could find friends to entertain with his caricatures of the meetings he grudgingly attended. But, gradually, he began to soften, to listen to stories that were always in some way like his own. He saw tougher guys than he was shed tears as they talked about losing their kids, abandoning their friends, betraying their wives and girlfriends.

As he began to risk sharing his own losses and his pervasive feelings of loneliness, he discovered what it was like to be genuinely close to other people and to be emotionally open with them.

Finding the Best Fit for Yourself

Now that you've read about some examples of community settings where you might want to practice new relational skills, let's begin the process of finding the best group or community for your initial explorations. This will be a slow process, one that will both guide and encourage you to experiment with finding the best kind of group or community for yourself.

Exercise

Assessing Your Interests and Comfort Zone

This is a three-part exercise. So, set aside about an hour to complete it. You can also come back to it later after you've had more time to think about it.

Part One: Make a list of all the groups or communities you have been involved with during your adult life. If it makes it easier, you can cluster related groups together under a single heading, for example, "Recreation" or "Spiritual" or "Support/Health Care." Don't worry about being orderly and don't try to itemize every single group. The point of the exercise is to create a map of where you've been and what types of groups you're most likely to choose.

Part Two: Circle the category or clustered activities where you think you're likely to feel most comfortable engaging in the relational experiments of Step Three. Now think about whether there might be a group or activity that might appeal to you, but that you haven't tried before. Add that to your list. Finally, put a star next to any group or community that you've tried before but found too difficult. If you think you might like to try this one again (or a group like it), put a double star next to it.

After doing this exercise, you'll have set up some possibilities to explore. This way of organizing what you have already experienced, along with some new group activities you might be willing to try, will help you match your Step Three starting point with what is most likely to work for you.

Part Three: Now, you need to think about your emotional comfort level. If you're someone who does better when you feel really challenged, you might decide that pursuing something that's completely new will give you the jolt you need to get going. But if you're likely to become anxious and back off when something is too new and different, this may not be your best choice for practicing new ways to relate to others.

Perhaps you'll choose to try your new relational skills in a group or community you've experienced before, but with a new set of goals and a new mind-set. If you do your best when you feel safest, you would probably choose to practice your new skills in a group that's the most familiar and comfortable. Distancers respond to new experiences in a variety of ways, so take your time in determining what setting will work the best for you.

This exercise was a real challenge for Rick, the sexual abuse survivor who kept himself safe by tightly controlling everything in his world. See whether "walking through" this exercise the way that Rick did will help you understand how this works.

Rick's Story

In getting started to do this work, Rick remembered that he had participated frequently in groups for recreational purposes, including a men's softball league, coaching his kids' soccer teams, and rock climbing with friends. He circled the category "recreation/sports" as what would feel the most ordinary and comfortable for him.

Next, he added the category of "spiritual" as a possible community he had considered exploring, but he hadn't pushed himself to try that yet. He thought a lot about returning to his church roots or finding a new spiritually centered group.

Finally, he put a star next to "family" as a community he had tried to be a part of in the past. Family had been difficult for him. He wasn't sure whether to mark this category with two stars, even though he wanted to become more fully a part of his family of origin and to feel closer to his current family. He considered developing a new set of goals and a new mind-set about what he wanted to happen with his family, but he realized it was just too anxiety-provoking. He just wasn't sure if he wanted to start out being so vulnerable, so he chose not to give this category two stars.

While thinking about these things, Rick contemplated his emotional comfort level. He knew he was someone who did well when challenged by something new. He thought about pursuing an involvement in some form of spirituality that would be new enough to challenge him to really invest time and energy in Step Three. On the other hand, he came to understand that he did not want to return to his childhood religious roots and that he was uncomfortable with the idea of something so far outside his experience as a meditation group. It would be "too different," he thought.

Then, he started feeling frustrated and angry about the whole idea of finding a group, and considered letting his life go on just the way it always had. At this point, he was about to give up, but then he remembered one of his buddies talking enthusiastically about martial arts. From what his friend had told him, he understood that if he got involved in this particular community, he could choose the comfort of engaging in a physical activity but also learn about a discipline with a more spiritual grounding.

After a few months of studying tae kwon do at the local dojo, Rick noticed some major changes in his pattern of controlling behavior. He began to feel less guarded and was becoming more comfortable with the experience of allowing his teacher to be in charge of the whole situation. As he experienced this new vulnerability, he became more open and more emotionally accessible without feeling that he had undergone a whole personality transplant. "I didn't feel as if it was the Invasion of the Body Snatchers *or anything like that," he told me, smiling a little, "but I did start to feel like a really different person. My wife and kids began to respond to the changes in how I related to them too. It was pretty cool." The longer he participated in the martial arts community, the more Rick's closeness with his wife continued to deepen and increase.*

Making Your Choice

Now you're ready to make your own list and to decide what kind of group or community will provide you with your best option. Keep in mind the purpose of this exercise is to help you figure out how to explore new dimensions of your relational repertoire in a way that will be both new and comfortable. Also, you should be entering a community or group that will work for you over time, so that you will gain the long-term benefits of your new affiliation.

Don't be surprised if at this point you want to back off and forget about Step Three. Risking change is always difficult, especially for distancers. Let's take another look at why this is a real challenge.

Why Distancers Hate Change

If you are really honest with yourself, you may discover that you just don't like taking new relational risks, period, whether in a group or not. There are plenty of reasons why you might want to end the journey you've been on right now and try to convince yourself you can live with everything in your relationship domain staying the same. As you know, the forces that shape our individual ways of approaching intimacy and challenge our comfort with intimacy are very powerful. It makes sense that if we risk new ways of connecting, we risk being vulnerable to old pain. We could be badly disappointed, hurt, betrayed, or trapped all over again. The temptation to stay away from such risks is often very strong.

Years ago, scientists studying animal behavior proved that if an animal keeps experiencing unpleasant responses to its actions, eventually, it will just give up and stop trying to change its situation: this is the condition called "learned helplessness." Our learned helplessness is another reason we may choose the misery we know rather than risk a new experience that potentially could lead to humiliation, heartbreak, or suffering. Distancers can get into this mode and become very comfortable with it because of their repetitive experiences of relational failures. It becomes habitual to give up and stop trying just as soon as we sense a shadow of anticipated pain.

Another reason to avoid taking action might be the belief that you already know all there is to know about yourself; you absolutely are sure about the parameters of what you like and don't like, what you will and won't do, what works and what doesn't. However, even though these notions may seem completely logical and sensible, the belief that you have nothing new to learn about yourself comes from a place of fear. Although there are, of course, some things you do know definitively about yourself—for example, you know you don't want to go hang gliding, or attend a Tupperware party, or live in a thatched hut in the Everglades—there are also many things you haven't explored that could enrich your life and teach you new relational skills. Keep in mind that you don't really know how a new venture might turn out once you have the right preparation and a new rationale for taking risks.

Refreshing and Expanding Your Survival Skills

Remember, this is your show. You can start out with whatever experiments for exploring community feel the most comfortable. You can make this a slow process. You don't have to push yourself into doing anything that feels too big and unmanageable. Think of yourself as a scientist studying new aspects of yourself. Let your curiosity lead you. You learned some new skills in earlier chapters. You'll be able to use them to help you try out new situations and new ways of being close to others. Before going any further, let's spend some time reviewing and expanding those skills.

Reviewing Mindfulness Skills

Throughout your work with the ARC model, you've had opportunities to practice mindfulness. Once again, you can use mindfulness to help you quell any anxieties you may be feeling about trying out new roles in new situations. You can even use your mindfulness skills to help you think about these new action challenges.

As you most likely remember, quieting your mind and body and focusing on the present moment are at the core of mindfulness practice. Instead of jumping ahead to how much you're going to hate being in a group or anticipating imagined failure in a new role, just remind yourself to stay in the present. Focus on your breath and observe any details around you that will help you to center yourself in the Now. You don't have to race forward or recall past mistakes, disappointments, humiliations, or pain.

Remember to use the breathing techniques that were introduced in chapter 2 when you began to deepen your awareness of your patterns in intimate relationships. You'll find that you can move yourself into just about any new situation with composure and a sense of calmness—if you focus on slowing and deepening your breathing. The more you practice this breathing technique, the more it will ground you in any new or distressing situation.

It's like managing pain. We now know that the secret of keeping pain from becoming unbearable is to contain it from its inception rather than toughing it out and letting it reach the number 10 (the standard hospital indication for unbearable pain on a scale of 1 to 10). As you work with the information and activities in Step Three, remember that you have the skills to stay in the present moment, and remember to calm your mind and body through deep breathing and focusing on the present moment.

Using the Mind-Body Connection

You can also tap into the mind-body connection you read about in chapter 2 as you face negative thoughts, self-doubt, and judgmental evaluations of others that will very likely arise while you begin to engage in new ways of relating. The body can be a great tool for changing the mind.

When you find yourself starting to make negative judgments against either yourself or others, try changing your body chemistry instead of trying to force yourself to think positive thoughts. Here are some ways you can do this:

- Before you enter a new group or situation, try to do some form of vigorous exercise that will get your heart pumping harder and your breathing faster. The amount of time you exercise will vary with your needs and your habits. One person might want to play a set of tennis first, while someone else might want to do sit-ups for ten minutes. When you finish exercising, you will then enter the new situation in a significantly calmer physical state, which also will change your body chemistry sufficiently to calm your mind.

- Try to break the train of thought that takes you down the mental path of dread or negative energy. You can change your mental channel by taking a hot shower or bath, or listening to music you like. Work at an activity that gets your body into sync with your mind like gardening, giving your dog a bath, or doing something creative that fully engages your mind and body. For example, make a painting, a bookshelf, a complicated recipe; fix a car engine, or repair an appliance.

- If you feel yourself becoming frustrated or angry at the thought of trying out a new group or activity that you think you're going to completely hate doing, try to do something physical that will release your anxiety-driven anger. You could drive around in your car—keeping the windows rolled up!—and shout at the top of your lungs. Or try punching pillows or shadow boxing. You could write a letter about what a stupid idea this group experiment is. Or call a friend to tell her why you are really furious about having to do this.

These are just a few ideas, but you get the picture. The key is to change your mental and emotional energy by changing your body chemistry. When I'm anxious or angry or frustrated or bored, I take a walk. It rarely fails me, and so I've learned how to prepare myself for walking in almost any climate or on any trip. Even in an unsafe area, I can usually walk on the treadmill in a hotel, or find a mall to walk around. I know from much practice that changing my physiological state automatically helps me ease into a better mental and emotional place.

Surrendering Control

Being able to surrender control is a skill that's often the hardest to learn. It certainly is the one that I continue to struggle with. Yet it actually can be the easiest, because when you take a longer look at whatever happens to be up for you, you will realize that you're not really in control of most situations to begin with.

Letting Go

It will help you to begin the process of finding a community to engage with by recognizing that surrendering control over the outcome of a venture is something you routinely practice. Let's take the example of surrendering control when you are stuck in a traffic jam. You can't move until the traffic starts moving, so you have to surrender control of the outcome, which is staying on your own personal schedule, or you will drive yourself crazy, have an attack of road rage, hold others hostage on your cell phone while you complain about the traffic jam, or otherwise spin your wheels mentally and emotionally.

Think about how you can surrender your efforts to mentally control the situation you are anticipating. No matter how carefully you try to control how the new group or event or role will turn out, control over the outcome is an illusion. You can't control the variables that other people will present, whatever they may or may not do. Then there's the unpredictability of how you may respond to any number of scenarios. Again, the more you allow yourself to surrender control of outcomes, the less you will be frustrated or disappointed by whatever transpires.

Surrendering control is especially important when you begin to practice new ways of being in intimate relationships. Trying to control what others do or say is almost always an exercise in futility; we all know this even if we sometimes forget it. So here's your chance to practice letting go by starting out with surrendering control within a group context.

Choosing Your Targets for Change

There are certain relational challenges that most distancers need to target in whatever groups or communities they select to learn their new relational skills.

Exercise

Targeting Relational Challenges

Use the following list to note the challenges you think are most relevant to yourself, rating the top five in order of their importance to you:

- Taking risks in sharing feelings and self-disclosure
- Letting go of being in control of others
- Prioritizing one-to-one relationships (within the group)
- Avoiding old patterns of approach-avoidance, that is, sticking with the group or community as opposed to dropping out or switching from one group to another
- Noticing and decreasing judgmental attitudes toward others
- Letting go of goal-oriented focus when relating to others
- Practicing cooperation
- Setting appropriate boundaries
- Overcoming fear of new people
- Using honest, direct communication instead of sarcasm or an indirect style

Matching Target Challenges to Community

When you've targeted the relational challenges you're going to start working on, you may want to do a little planning as to how you will proceed in the community or group you select. Your course of action may seem immediately obvious, or you may feel puzzled about how this is going to work. Let's use an example of another distancer's experience to illustrate how this works. By going through the details of what happened to Janine, you can watch someone experience what you are about to do, and come out okay at the end.

Janine's Story

As you may recall, Janine had begun to develop more trust in relationships when she got involved in a women's group for trauma survivors at the local women's community drop-in center. There she was able to become vulnerable enough to allow other women to get to know her. She discovered after months of participating in groups at the women's center that she could trust the other women not to betray her trust or to blame her for her past suffering.

She still wanted to work on some other problematic areas of relationship, and she chose to prioritize letting go of the illusion that she could control what others might do, say, or think. She had also chosen "spiritual-based community" as the new social group she really wanted to explore. She knew she didn't want to return to the church affiliation she had grown up with, but she felt drawn to meditation groups.

Janine learned to meditate in my Addictions and Trauma Recovery Model group (ATRIUM) for trauma survivors at the women's center. Meditation made her feel much more peaceful both mentally and physically, and she was hoping that she would begin to feel more connected at a spiritual level. So she joined a meditation group that a woman at the center had recommended. It was open to anyone who wanted to drop in, unlike some meditation groups that required introductory training.

Janine wasn't sure this would be the best place to practice letting go of her fear of others and her pattern of judging others before she even got to know them. How can you practice these skills in a group where there is very little action, and conversation is kept at a minimum? Nonetheless, she felt safest when she thought about risking her new relational practices here, and the group met her need for a community that might become a long-term source of nurturance and support. To her surprise, she found she was able to work on her goals sooner than she expected.

Many people in the meditation group went out for breakfast in the late morning after the meditation session ended. They invited Janine to join them, and putting aside her usual fear of new people, she did. It soon became clear that there were many ways in which she was still judging how safe others were and holding herself back. She wanted to control who she sat down next to, whose friendly questions she answered, and how many people squeezed in together at the little tables in the nearby coffee shop.

Janine especially wanted to avoid contact with one man who irritated her in every way. She disliked his scraggly beard, his scent (sweat with an overlay of wood smoke), and his self-confident friendliness. He often sat next to her, and seemed to have no qualms about asking her personal questions. Worse still, he often insisted on telling her all about how the meditation had gone for him, including the details of how comfortable (or not) his back and knees had been during the hour of silent sitting on cushions. She disliked everything about him, including his weird name, Wyatt.

Reminding herself that her discomfort offered her exactly what she was there to practice changing, she calmed herself by breathing deeply, and gradually began to be less judgmental toward the group and even toward Wyatt. One morning she came close to tears after a deep meditative experience when she had the powerful experience of feeling her beloved grandmother's presence. Her grandmother had died the previous winter and Janine was still grieving her loss. When Wyatt squeezed in beside her at the coffee shop, she was ready to get up and leave.

"Hey," he said, "what's up? You look really sad, or something."

Janine reminded herself that she was practicing new ways of being closer to people, even to Wyatt. So, she took another deep breath, coughing slightly as she breathed in Wyatt's sweat and wood smoke scents and said, "I am sad."

Wyatt surprised her by not asking why. He just took her hand in his and held it. It felt surprisingly okay. They sat there for what seemed like hours to Janine. After her initial discomfort, she discovered she didn't mind holding his hand. She even noticed that she didn't want to pull her hand away. After a while he said, "Your tea is probably cold by now. I'll get you another cup. Ginger peach, right?" He took her cold drink, and returned quickly with a cup of hot tea.

They ended up staying in the coffee shop long after the others left. Wyatt didn't try to comfort her with words, but he listened carefully to everything that she told him through her tears about her grandmother. "She sounds like she was one cool lady," he said at the end of their conversation. After that day, Janine began to feel much less alone and she found that she was enjoying getting closer to Wyatt and the others in the meditation group.

Staying the Course with Your New Experiment

Not everyone has Janine's luck in matching their choice of group and their target relational challenges. Sometimes you have to work at it for quite a while to pull it all together. If your experiment starts to unravel despite your best efforts to plan carefully, Ben's story may help you to feel less alone.

Ben's Story

Ben decided that he would work on his relational challenges within the community of his condo association. His condo was in a beautiful old building in the country. Built in the nineteenth century by affluent New England seekers who believed that a simple life in the country was the only healthy way to live, it had once been a utopian community. The rambling three-story building had been turned into condominiums in the 1980s. Although the buildings and the land were lovely to look at, there were a host of structural problems for the condo dwellers.

Ben made the decision to take a leadership role in getting the old building's structural problems repaired, and to use this opportunity to work on the relationships he was slowly forming with the other residents. He had decided to prioritize deepening one-to-one relationships within the group, and to stick with the group through the good and bad times rather than following his old approach-avoidance pattern in relationships. He also changed his usual skittish style by concentrating his energies on this one group rather than having several other new ventures lined up as soon as he began to feel restless.

He chose the condo association as the best setting for his Step Three work because it was the type of community he had always wanted to be part of, despite some previous failures. He gave it two stars to indicate that it was the kind of community he wanted to try again. He believed it would be both comfortable enough and challenging enough to meet his requirements.

As he got more deeply involved in the condo project, he began to focus on deepening his relationships with a few individuals who were also very active in the condo association. Not only did he accept invitations to spend long work sessions and social time with them in a group, he also spent time with people individually, inviting them to dinner at his place and accepting invitations to social events.

Within a few months he began to feel overwhelmed. He enjoyed his new friendships with several of the other condo residents, but he was starting to feel pressured by one of the women. He wondered whether she wanted a romantic relationship with him when she invited him for dinner and to a play in the nearest city. Despite his qualms, he pushed himself to go ahead since he had committed himself to stay steady and not run when relationships deepened.

Ben had recognized he was becoming increasingly judgmental toward Belinda as she had increased her invitations to meet with him, even before her invitation to attend the play. She seemed to be turning into a weak and helpless stereotypic female, not at all the person he had originally admired in their meetings with plumbers, carpenters, and electricians.

The night they went to the city, Ben was extremely uncomfortable. He couldn't enjoy the play and he began to feel claustrophobic. He wondered if he had inadvertently replicated the old toxic dynamics of his childhood. At the end of the evening when they sat in the car outside their condo building, he felt as though Belinda were holding him hostage. It was late, and Ben was miserable as he sat listening to her talk about problems at her job and her increasing loneliness since she had moved into the condo. The tipping point came when she turned to Ben, and said, "Ben, I don't know what I would do without you. You're one of the only friends I've made since I moved out here. You really are some kind of miracle in my life."

After that night, Ben politely backed away from the pressure he felt from Belinda. He began to avoid her and decided he would drop out of the condo repair project. He also began looking for another place to live.

In our therapy sessions, we focused on creating another option for Ben, working together to see whether this time he could manage to stick with a relationship and not let it trigger his runaway pattern. He had been enjoying the community effort, he liked where he lived, and he was happy to have deepened his friendships with the other people he had been getting to know. Finally, he forced himself to talk to Belinda, to tell her how he was feeling and why.

To his surprise, she was very comfortable with his disclosures about his runaway patterns in his relationships with women, his need to stay free of any demands, and his classic fears of being consumed by female loneliness. She began to share some information about her own patterns of sabotaging close relationships, her wish to have the kind of intimate relationship that she had experienced with her sisters in childhood. Like Ben, she longed for a relationship that would provide for all her emotional needs.

After a while, Ben and Belinda became good friends. They were able to help each other work on the relational challenges each faced. They discussed their expectations of the perfect romantic relationship. Belinda was able to help Ben practice being more relaxed about his relational safety boundaries. Eventually, when Belinda got into a serious relationship with a man she'd met at work, Ben was happy for her. He also realized he would miss her if she left the condo to move closer to her new partner.

It was a cause for celebration when Ben was able to tell Belinda about his fear of losing her, without going into a panic that she would drop her new relationship and come running to him with a new rush of expectations. The following summer Ben cheerfully participated in her wedding and welcomed her new husband into their condo "family."

Just Do It!

Now, you have all the tools you need to take the plunge and get started. You've done the preparation that will give you the best opportunity to choose the group or community where you are most likely to succeed. You've given yourself some specific relational challenges to work on, and you've read the accounts of other distancers who worked at Step Three and succeeded. You're good to go!

You also should plan to take notes regularly on the significant moments and encounters that occur throughout your practice of Step Three. Use your journal. Observe whether there are patterns that you need to pay attention to or to change.

Try to find someone to talk to about this phase of your work. You should try to explain as well as you can what this work is all about for you. Let your confidant know what your goals are, why you chose this particular group or community, and how long you're planning to conduct this experiment.

As you plan your new venture, remember to give yourself a reasonable timeline for how long you will conduct your experiment. For example, you may want to give yourself three months. This means that if things are really not working out, you can stop and try to find a different community to engage with to do Step Three work.

Assessing Your Progress

Make a commitment to stick with your chosen group for at least several months, knowing that you will undoubtedly feel a variety of discomforts during the early stages of your new activity. The most predictable response you might have to the new situation would be "I feel really uncomfortable in this group. This is really not going to work for me." This response is very likely to disturb your thoughts and feelings when you join a group that's new to you. You also might feel this discomfort even in a group you're already part of as you get involved at a deeper level and start to connect with others in a deeper way. If this happens, instead of giving in to your distress, think about what you might do with your reaction.

One way to deal with it might be to tell yourself that if it wasn't somewhat uncomfortable for you, then you probably aren't really digging into the work of Step Three. If you find that you're very comfortable with a new situation, that's not a good sign. It's either not different enough for you to try out new behavior, or you're not really allowing yourself to enter the experience.

Here's an example of how one distancer moved himself out of his comfort zone after he recognized that he wasn't really doing the work he wanted to be doing.

Andrew's Story

Remember Andrew? He's the fellow who had so much trouble settling into any relationship because he was always zooming around and never allowing himself to really land anywhere. When Andrew got to Step Three, he decided to stick with the community that was the most important to him as well as the most familiar, the meeting rooms of Alcoholics Anonymous. But he decided to practice getting closer to individuals within the program and to try to stay steady within those relationships rather than following his old patterns of running away the minute he began to feel he was getting too close to anyone.

After a few months, though, he discovered that he had chosen a group that was too familiar, too comfortable, and that he wasn't really experiencing the kinds of changes he knew could lead him to greater success in establishing intimacy. So he went back to the drawing board and decided to try something a bit more challenging that would allow him to develop his new skills more successfully. He looked at his list and thought again about his on-again off-again relationship to the church community he had grown up in. He made the decision to reopen his connection with his local parish.

Finally, Andrew succeeded in making a big change in his relational patterns by volunteering to work with a group of church members that did outreach to inactive local parishioners to determine how the church could become more relevant in their lives.

As he learned to sit and really listen to the people he visited, he began to slow himself down little by little. He often went on these visits with other volunteers from the group. One of them, a man much older than Andrew, talked to him about how long it had taken him to get to a place of real comfort in his own life. One day Andrew realized that he had been sitting and talking with his new friend for two hours without even feeling restless.

It was a quantum leap for Andrew to find out that he was capable of sitting for hours with another person engaged in a conversation that was personal and that also made him feel vulnerable. He began to discover that the more he practiced doing this, the more relaxed he became with everyone who crossed his path.

Monitoring Your Progress

So, after going through the usual ups and downs of the first three months of your brave new experiment, how will you determine if things are moving along in an okay way? You can use the following exercises to help you decide whether you really need to change gears and try some other group or community, or whether you need to revise your target relational goals and challenges.

Exercise

Monitoring Negative Effects

Use this scale:

1 = This doesn't describe me at all.
2 = This describes my behavior a little bit.
3 = This describes my behavior in some ways.
4 = This describes quite a lot of my behavior.
5 = This is definitely me!

Rate yourself from 1 to 5 to answer the following statements:

1. I feel overwhelmed by the amount of time I'm devoting to my new group/community. ______
2. I dread going each time I participate in the new group/community. ______
3. I feel like an outsider. ______
4. I feel lonelier than before I began this new group/activity. ______
5. I don't seem to have much in common with the others in this group. ______
6. I'm using ____________ (relevant addiction or bad health habit) more than before I started attending this group. ______
7. I am not feeling well (tired, aches and pains, etc.) since getting involved in this group/community. ______
8. I feel increasingly hopeless about my ability to change my way of relating to others. ______
9. I think I was better off in general before I started Step Three. ______
10. I still need others to relate to me on my terms. ______

If your score is high (anything above 40), you may want to think about finding a different kind of group, community, or activity.

If your score is midrange (between 30 and 40), think about reassessing the target behaviors you've been working on. Maybe the group itself is right for you, but you're trying to do something that's too challenging at this time. Try scaling down your expectations. And before you make any big changes, do the following exercise, to see how to look for positive changes. You may be surprised.

Exercise

Monitoring Positive Effects

Use this scale:

1 = This doesn't describe me at all.
2 = This describes my behavior a little bit.
3 = This describes my behavior in some ways.
4 = This describes quite a lot of my behavior.
5 = This is definitely me!

Rate yourself from 1 to 5 to answer the following statements:

1. I like the people I'm getting to know in the new group/ community. _____
2. I look forward to group activities/meetings. _____
3. My friends and/or family have been noticing positive changes in me over the past three months. _____
4. I feel hopeful about how I'm handling new relational experiences. _____
5. I am feeling less lonely. _____
6. I'm feeling more energy physically. _____
7. I notice that I'm more able to let others relate to me on their terms. _____

8. I am being more open and honest with people about how I feel. ______

9. I'm dealing with conflict more directly. ______

10. I'm curious about what will happen next in my life. ______

If your score is high (anything above 40), you are probably doing just what you need to do, and you have found a group or community that is working well for you.

If your score is midrange (between 30 and 40), try changing some of the target behaviors you've been working on. Maybe you're trying the wrong things or trying too many things at once. The group itself may be fine, but you could challenge yourself a little more.

If your score is under 25, it's very likely time to find a different group or community, and take the pressure off yourself trying to make this one work.

This is a very important period of your life, a time to try out new situations, to assess if they're working, and to try again if the first choice isn't right. Above all, be kind to yourself during this process. This is a very big project, and nothing is going to fall into place quickly. Give yourself time, and remember that you have nothing to lose. The exciting thing is that you have no idea where this adventure may take you, and who you will find yourself with as you learn to change your relationships. Just keep breathing!

In chapter 6, you will move into doing some work within the couple relationship, either with your current partner or in quest of a partner. There's no rush to move to this last phase of your journey. In the meantime, give yourself time to really explore and enjoy your success in making community connections. This is the work of a lifetime and you're doing it!

6 Step Three, Part Two: Changing Your Relationships

You have reached the final challenge, the step that will give you what you've been seeking. Now you are ready to move forward into the process of working at improving your intimate relationships. To help you with this work, you have new information, new relational skills, and an expanded network of support. You have greatly increased your capacity to risk the vulnerabilities and joys of love. Most important, you are not alone—you have a variety of support options, including the wisdom of others who have been where you've been and who have all improved their relational and intimacy skills.

Preparing Yourself for Success

Let's get started by reviewing what you've learned about yourself in preparation for this last important step. You can meet this last challenge because of all the preparation you've been doing to arrive at this point.

Knowing Yourself

As you approach the area of intimate relationships, you know who you are and what you're looking for. You've been figuring out the self-definition that best fits you; comparing and contrasting yourself with the other distancers whose stories you now know. Perhaps you've discovered that you distance yourself from intimacy by avoiding relationships; that is, you are a "disappearing distancer" like Andrew, Janine, or Julie. Or you've noticed that even though you can get into relationships, you play out the approach-avoidance tango of the "defended distancer," similar to Jack, who pursued unavailable partners, or Ben, who fled from one partner after another, or Diego, searching for the impossible dream of meeting someone who could meet all of his emotional needs. Maybe you defend yourself emotionally or sexually like Yvonne, Rick, or Danny. Maybe you recognize that you avoid communication vulnerability like Chris, who was afraid to risk difficult emotional exchanges with her partner Beth, or Luisa, who was fearful of her partner Diego's emotional openness.

You may have found a description like yours in the stories about Sally or Danny, and identified yourself as a "distracted distancer" so fully occupied by your work, family, or other people's crises that there is nothing left over for your couple relationship. Or maybe you're more like Colin, so involved in your addiction that you're too distracted from making meaningful relationships.

While you were learning to assess your style of distancing, your growing awareness created change. All you needed was the willingness to look at yourself in your moments of vulnerability. You learned that you could name a relationship pattern that describes and fits your individual history, and by doing that, you learned you were in good company. That must have been a terrifically liberating moment, recognizing that you are not uniquely isolated in your ways of relating to others and that many other women and men have faced the same challenges you have.

Recognizing Mutual Distancing Dynamics

You also have learned that partners sometimes can reinforce or inflame each other's distancing patterns. Remember how Diego and Luisa's marriage went under when they tried to confront their divergent communication styles? Each wanted the other to be radically different, and when they tried to force these changes, their marriage couldn't sustain the stress.

You learned from their story that being able to name the problem in an intimate relationship sometimes may lead to dissolution of the relationship. Ending relationships doesn't have to be viewed either as a failure or a tragedy. This book offers you the lesson that when a couple has irreconcilable differences in their visions of intimacy, they can't always sustain their relationship.

Now let's take a look at the new skills you have learned during the process of risking change.

Your New Relational Skills

As you worked on each step in the Awareness, Remembering, and Connecting (ARC) model, you gained new skills in your journey toward a fulfilling intimate relationship. Some of the assessment skills have guided you to a better understanding of your relational challenges and desires. You've also added new skills to your repertoire to help you engage in new situations and challenges, and to uncover the parts of your past that may need a deeper examination.

Exercise

Reviewing Skills

Below is a list of the basic skills you've been learning and practicing. As you review the list, pay attention to which of these skills have now become a part of your daily life and which ones could use a little more practice. Make one check mark next to the skills you use only occasionally, and then put two check marks next to the skills you use often. Some skills will probably remain unchecked, but be as honest with yourself as you can about this:

1. Breathing mindfully: learning to relax and allow your capacity for serenity to emerge to help you deal with difficult new situations and old ghosts ______
2. Identifying with others: letting yourself learn by contemplating others who share your behaviors and challenges ______
3. Rating yourself in those areas you need to explore and change ______
4. Valuing your strengths: noticing not only what needs to change, but what the strengths that you bring to your relationships are because of who you are and what you've been through ______
5. Examining specific aspects of your past relationship history in the service of understanding your present problems, hopes, and dreams ______
6. Consciously teaching yourself by instructing yourself to resist old mental and behavioral patterns ______
7. Consciously silencing memories of your past that are no longer useful ______
8. Tuning in to your body frequently to understand what's going on with you at all levels ______
9. Joining with others to make the changes you choose to make ______
10. Using your natural curiosity to learn more about how others in couple relationships relate to each other ______
11. Letting go of your illusion of control and taking some risks ______

How to use this exercise: Notice which skills you haven't been using much, and write a few notes for yourself about why you've been neglecting to practice using these tools. Also give yourself credit for what you have been doing. Circle the skills you especially want to use more.

As you look over this list, you may think of other new skills you've added since you began to work with this book. The new skills you've been gathering in your support networks and community or group endeavors are especially important.

Remember: In this last part of Step Three, you can trust these skills to help you whenever you approach your new ventures. You have a new capacity to risk closeness and vulnerability. You will not be permanently wounded. You do not have to do this alone. As Susan B. Anthony famously declared, "Failure is impossible!"

How to Begin Opening the Door to Intimacy

You are now going to put into action all that you've been learning and practicing since you first began working with this book and the ARC model. You are ready to start the process of making changes in the area of intimacy within a couple relationship. Let's talk about how to make this process work best.

First, let's begin with some general guidelines. The following apply whether you are just starting the process of approaching potential partners or are making changes in your long-term couple relationship.

Guidelines for Making Successful Changes

- **Set small goals.** The worst mistake most people make when they are trying out something new and frightening is to immediately go for the gold; that is, for the finish line at the end of the race, when they really should begin with a walk to the corner. Obviously, this guideline will be very different in action for each person.

For example, if you are a disappearing distancer, you would want to try talking to that special person for a little while longer, or at a slightly more personal level of conversation, instead of asking him or her to go away for a weekend with you. Or suppose you've been addicted to your exercise routine, but you've decided to work on spending more time with someone special and less time exercising. It would be much more sensible to give up one exercise session in the week, rather than go cold turkey and totally quit your whole exercise routine in order to spend every night with Ms. or Mr. Right.

- **Focus on changes you can make right now.** Don't focus on something you hope will happen someday at the end of your relational journey. If you plan to work on opening up a little bit more emotionally, start with one small part of yourself that you feel is ready to be shared, rather than going for a full range of emotional vulnerability right away. It's important to take your time when you are aiming at big changes.

- **Prioritize safety.** Begin with target behaviors and people who you feel are relatively safe. If you're a defended distancer and you're making a commitment to hang in there with a new relationship, even if things are feeling a little too intense and intimate, don't lock yourself into something too risky. Don't go from a standstill to moving in together, or to getting engaged, or going off together on a long trip to a romantic island.

  For the distracted distancer who is ready to let go of an all-consuming addiction to make some space for a partner, move toward withdrawal from your addiction in a planned way, giving yourself plenty of support and time for recovery before fully offering yourself to another person.

- **Think of your first steps as experiments.** Remember that nothing you do is final. You will probably have to explore lots of new behaviors and situations before you become really comfortable with the new you. If you view what you're doing as an experiment, you can take both successes and setbacks in your stride: it's all just information.

  If you decide to try harder to meet potential partners, don't give up if your efforts don't bear fruit right away. This is just a way to deepen your understanding of yourself while you try out new relational options. Nothing that happens will be all bad or all good, so don't be overconcerned with evaluating your efforts.

- **Stay tuned in to the wisdom of your body.** At first, you will probably find that you feel awkward, nervous, unsure of what's happening. You may feel lost and confused. Don't overthink. Trust your body to give you feedback. If the situation you're exploring makes your body feel jittery, that's to be expected. But if your body keeps sending huge warning alarms, pay attention. It may mean that this is the wrong activity or wrong person for you at this time.

- **Keep your sense of humor.** You know things are never really smooth when you're trying out anything new, so prepare yourself to feel foolish. Just keep in touch with that part of you that can see humor in your most dismal efforts, and remember, we have all been there.

- **Stay connected to your support people.** As you engage in these new efforts, be sure to stay connected to those who support you. Talk to others about what you're planning to do, how it's going, and what the next step is looking like.

- **Set timelines for your plans.** You need to create a structure that will tell you when you're going to begin something new, how long you're going to try it, and if it doesn't work out, when you'll let it go and try something else. In general, setting up relatively short amounts of time, like a month or so, helps you feel less overwhelmed by new ways of doing things. For people with addictions, it often works best if they commit themselves to stay abstinent just one day at a time. Whatever you choose, try to stay with it for the allotted time.

Disappearing Distancers: Getting Started

If you've determined that you're a disappearing distancer, then you know your major task is to put yourself into more "dating" situations. Or you may prefer to think about it as inviting yourself out into the world of available single people. How will you get over your fears, shyness, and self-doubt, and begin to do this?

The first question to ask yourself is what kind of person would you like to get to know? You can then think about the best ways to get acquainted with such people.

Or perhaps you already know someone you find attractive. The question for you is "How can I get to know this person better?"

Janine's Story

Janine is a good role model for this category of distancer. She started by getting to know other women who had been dealing with similar challenges through participating in the ATRIUM group (Addictions and Trauma Recovery Model group) at the women's community resource center. Then she took the risk of exploring a weekly meditation group where she got to know a variety of new people, including her friend Wyatt.

The next level of risk-taking for Janine was to initiate further contact with Wyatt outside of the weekly meditation group meetings. She wanted to feel safe, and not push herself to do anything too big too soon. When she thought about inviting Wyatt over to her apartment for a meal, her body told her in no uncertain terms that this was way too scary. Her stomach began hurting, and at the same time she felt cravings for some unhealthy snack foods that she had been successfully avoiding for more than a year. So, then she chose to use some of her support people to discuss her intentions. She met with several other women who she knew had more experience than she did with early dating options.

When Janine first invited Wyatt to do something alone with her, separate from the meditation group, she asked him if he wanted to go to a lecture given by a Tibetan meditation teacher. She had to laugh at herself when Wyatt readily agreed to it but suggested that they go with some of the other people from the morning coffee group.

Her next effort was a little more spontaneous. One beautiful morning she asked Wyatt if he wanted to go for a walk with her after the morning coffee gathering. She suggested taking a beautiful walk through the woods not far from where they met every week. Off they went, and to her delight it turned out that Wyatt could identify every birdcall they heard along the way, and even tried to imitate some especially tricky ones. By the end of the walk, they were laughing and relaxing with each other.

It was not hard to invite him to come for dinner the next time she saw him. But it took many months before she felt safe enough to want to become sexually intimate with him. She was able to tell Wyatt about her past experience of being raped. They talked for hours after she told him. Eventually, following a series of conversations, Janine gradually became able to be more physically comfortable with Wyatt. When they finally made love, it felt as easy and as safe as it had the first day he had held her hand when she'd cried about her grandmother.

For most fearful and shy distancers, things may not go quite as smoothly as they did for Janine. Here are a few tips to help you keep going:

- Give yourself permission to go as slowly as you want. You can think for weeks about who you want to approach before you act on your idea. And once you start initiating contact with other single people, don't feel that you have to turn it into a full-time activity. Pace yourself. Take the time to enjoy the small successes when they happen and to heal from the disappointments that may also occur.

- Try to line up a "coach" from among your support people, someone who can persuade you to keep going when you want to give up. Make sure you call your coach when you're going to initiate contact with someone special. Also make a plan to talk to your coach as soon as possible after you've met this person, e-mailed, gone out with him or her, or whatever. Your coach doesn't really have to tell you what to do. What you need is someone to remind you that you're doing great and to just keep going and trust yourself.

- Don't put all your eggs into one basket. You will very likely have to try making connections with a number of people before you find someone you really like, that special person with whom you share compatibility and a mutual attraction. This is when it will be helpful to remember that you're engaging in an experiment. First-time success is not that likely, but everything you try out to practice your new skills will provide you with useful information.

- Don't evaluate the new relationship or the person too quickly. Remember that you are probably also looking for any excuse to go back to the safety of your single safe life. Give yourself enough time and information about any new people to be absolutely sure before you cross them off your list of possibilities.

- Don't settle for someone you don't feel really comfortable with just to have a relationship. You've waited quite a while to approach this world of intimacy, so take your time. Trust yourself to know when a relationship feels really good to you. And keep using your support people to help you with this.

They can help you determine what's working in your new relationship and what's not.

- Listen to the other person's fears, doubts, and hesitations. This is an important part of beginning a new relationship. You may not be the only distancer in this couple. Don't get defensive and give up if the other person doesn't jump into a relationship with you immediately. But don't run away either.

The Defended Distancer Opens the Door

If you are currently single, and you identify yourself as a defended distancer, let's first take a look at what you might want to consider doing. This time around you have a much better chance of starting a relationship that just might work out for you. You can begin by doing the following exercise. It will help you move mindfully toward the person who would be right for you. When you can hold a picture in your mind of who you want to be and what kind of person would make you feel most fully present and healthy, this exercise will help you connect with that person.

Exercise

Visualizing Your Ideal Relationship

Give yourself enough time and space to do this exercise. Make sure you won't be distracted or interrupted for at least thirty minutes. Choose a comfortable place to sit, and if it helps you to stay relaxed and to focus, use some background music or sounds from nature, such as ocean waves or birdsongs.

Now give yourself the instruction to visualize yourself with someone who could be that special person you've been hoping for. Picture the two of you doing a routine, simple task together. It could be any kind of activity a couple who've been together for a while might do, like shopping for groceries, having dinner, watching a video, or taking a walk. Try not to become preoccupied with what this person looks like; instead, concentrate on how the two of you interact with each other.

Your answers to the following questions will help you fill in some important details of the picture you are creating in your mind of yourself and this other person:

- How does this person make you feel?
- Can you imagine yourself and this person hanging out with some of the important people in your life? Do they like him/her?
- What would it be like to just relax with this person? Do you feel safe, comfortable? Is either one of you trying to make the other happy? Can you picture yourself telling him/her some of your most cherished dreams/memories? Can you see yourselves laughing together?
- Can you imagine telling this person that you need some "alone" time for yourself and having that need be okay for each of you?
- Can you picture the two of you together when you're older? Can you imagine being there for this person when he/she is sick in bed with a bad cold and in a foul mood?
- Can you imagine listening to the details of this person's daily life? Do you think he/she would be interested in hearing about your daily life?

Spend at least thirty minutes exploring this fantasy and take as much additional time as you might want to do it. Then, in your journal, write a few notes about your visualization. Make time to share your fantasy with someone in your support circle, and be honest about what you learned from doing this exercise.

Making Your Game Plan

Now it's time to make a plan that will help you find the kind of person you've been picturing. Consider your usual pattern of getting into a relationship for a while. Try to avoid your old pitfalls, like seeking out partners based on their glamour or success or dazzle power. Where could you find someone who would be most likely to have the personality and the kind of interests you visualized in the "ideal couple" exercise above? What kinds of shared interests might bring you together?

After you finish all this work, relax. Sometimes you just can't know for sure what will turn out to be the right door for you to open. Jack's story illustrates how a twist of fate can lead to a welcome surprise.

Jack and Celia's Story

Jack was all too aware of his tendency to pursue unavailable women. So he decided to take it easy and wait for someone just to happen across his path in the new life he had chosen to live after he quit his job at the university. He fantasized the woman he hoped to meet might be another artist, someone he might even meet in the building where he was renting studio space.

He was taking care of a friend's dog for a week and enjoying the walks they took together beside the river near his condo. One day, from out of nowhere, a large rambunctious puppy appeared on the path and began trying to play with Jack's dog. His dog growled menacingly, but the puppy continued to bounce joyfully around the older dog. Jack became annoyed. Where was this puppy's owner?

A woman came trotting along the path, breathlessly calling out to the puppy. "Wally!" she shouted, "come here!" She apologized to Jack as she rescued his dog from her puppy's rapturous overtures. "I'm so sorry," she said, "he's still a puppy and he got away from me just now. I hope you and your dog are okay."

Jack reassured her that his canine companion was an old codger who no longer enjoyed the attentions of young dogs. He thought no more about the woman and her dog, but the following day they met again on the river path, this time without their dogs. They walked along together a little way until they came to the spot where they both had parked their cars. To Jack's consternation, he discovered he must have dropped his car keys somewhere along the path. He was going to be late for a meeting with a gallery owner, a woman he knew to be difficult. Jack's new walking companion offered to give him a lift to his appointment. She insisted on waiting for him while he met with "She-who-must-be-obeyed" (as Jack called the gallery owner), and then drove him back to the path where they soon found his lost keys.

Jack didn't know that he was at the beginning of a new friendship with Celia, another distancer, whom you met in chapter 1. (Remember? Celia had been so busy with her real estate business that she never had time for a relationship.) When they met, Celia was trying to change her life to make room for relationships, so it was a lucky coincidence that she met Jack when she did. Ordinarily, the last thing she would've done was to make time to help someone in the middle of her busy workday. But the new Celia was en route to leaving loneliness behind, so she took the time to help Jack.

Jack was intrigued by Celia. She seemed to him to have an openness that was unusual in his experience of women. They ended up talking for a long time, comparing notes on self-employment and the creative life.

One thing led to another. Jack and Celia eventually became lovers, each finding new ways to be present in the relationship. They agreed they were content to continue living apart, and to honor the time each needed separate from their couple relationship. Celia was able to continue spending the time needed to keep her business going, but she and Jack talked on the phone and e-mailed each other between their times together. Jack discovered that he was no longer compelled to be the pursuer, but neither was he being rejected. Celia was very warm and loving, and the time she wanted to spend with him was always freely given. What was especially notable was that, as Celia remained available and loving, Jack didn't pull away, as he would have done previously.

Monitoring Relational Problem Areas

Whether you are currently single, or trying to change your patterns of defended distancing in a current relationship, there are several important areas to monitor if you want to walk into the sunset with a loved one this time around.

Send the Right Signals

It's critically important for you to notice what kind of signals or messages you're sending the person you're just inching toward or getting involved with. Are you promising more availability than you actually will be able to deliver? Do you appear to be confident and relationally relaxed when in fact you're struggling with your fear of intimacy? It's important to be as open with your partner as is possible this time.

Ben's Story

When Ben was ready to approach a new relationship with the still-deepening understanding of himself as a defended distancer, he began to be more honest with the women he was seeing.

At first, he was overwhelming in his determination to show all his relational cards. He spent one entire evening telling someone he had just met about his efforts to stop promising what he had trouble delivering. He went into painful detail about the women he had previously harmed through his lack of honesty about his ambivalence and fear of commitment. The woman never went out with him again, and she refused to answer his phone calls. He learned from a mutual acquaintance that she had referred to him as "that nutball." After that painful experience, Ben began to be more careful about his degree of self-disclosure.

Ben was learning to pay attention to what he heard himself promising. Whenever he had doubts about the likelihood of his following through on plans, commitments, or emotional sharing, he would stop himself and take some time to rethink what he was communicating. If he had blundered and promised more than was comfortable for him, he learned to apologize but to also clarify what was realistic for him.

Guidelines for Self-Awareness

Ben gave himself three guidelines to follow. They also may be helpful for you. When in doubt, ask yourself the following questions:

1. Am I communicating what I really want to offer, or am I promising something I think the other person wants from me?
2. Am I being honest in general about the person I "advertise" myself as being?
3. Am I being honest with myself?

Slowing Down Your Inner Judge

Keep your tendency to look for imperfection in check by monitoring your critical, evaluative voice. That is, don't jump too quickly to evaluate the other person or the relationship. Remind yourself that you may not be evaluating correctly because of your fear of being hurt, suffocated, or disappointed. Work on staying as open as you can for as long as you can.

People rarely give you an accurate sense of who they truly are at first. Most people either overplay certain characteristics or disguise themselves in the nervous start-up of a new relationship. Almost all people turn out to be more complicated than their initial presentation of themselves once you get to know them better.

Holding Your Ground

You know that part of your pattern as a defended distancer is to have one foot out the door when you're getting close to someone. You are poised for flight. You zoom in and out of an intimate relationship like a wild creature snatching morsels of food before fleeing to safety. This time around, though, you are going to practice keeping your seat. This will work best if you target small situations or interactions where you will stay with what's happening longer than you would have in the past.

Gradually, you'll become able to increase your steadiness for longer amounts of time, and to extend your steady presence, even in the face of more intense relational demands. Just keep telling yourself that you can get through your panic and desire to flee. You may need to reassure yourself that if the situation were to become truly threatening to your mental health and emotional safety, you would know enough to get out.

Danny's Story

Danny, the young science-fiction writer, was relatively oblivious to the fear and anxiety that permeated his relationship with his girlfriend Roxy. He kept a chasm of emotional distance between the two of them without recognizing how careful he was to keep himself safe from loss. Anytime things began to get a bit more serious between them, Danny used a plausible excuse to leave for a while. Roxy was too afraid of losing him or scaring him off to call him on his flight pattern.

It was Danny's older brother who finally got through to him. Nick waited for Danny to finish explaining why he and Roxy weren't going away for the weekend as they'd planned to do. Nick shook his head at his brother, while telling him, "Danny, you're full of it! You do this every time you and Roxy start to get closer. You've cancelled so many trips with her I don't know why she keeps on seeing you. What's up with you?"

Danny was puzzled. He hadn't noticed this pattern, and if anyone had asked him, he would have said that his relationship with Roxy was terrific. "I don't know what you're talking about," he replied, looking at his brother in genuine bewilderment.

"Here's what I think," Nick told him. "Either you're too lazy to break up with Roxy and look for someone you could really go for, or you're scared. I think you're really scared." Although Nick thought

he knew what his younger brother was afraid of, he hoped Danny would figure it out for himself.

The next morning Danny was waiting outside Roxy's apartment when she came out the front door to go to work. He had a cup of coffee and her favorite scone ready as he invited her to take a ride with him before going to work. "We need to talk," he said. "Get in. I'll drive you."

In a few minutes he had summarized Nick's questions and his own thoughts about the matter. "I guess maybe I am scared," he confided, "but I don't know what's scaring me. I really love you. You know that, don't you?"

Roxy was a brave young woman and she didn't want to lose him. "Danny," she said gently, "I'm just guessing here, but I feel that your mother's death is the elephant in the room. We never talk about it. You and your brother never talk about it. You were so young when you lost her. Do you think you're afraid you'll lose me if we get too close?"

Although Danny took some time to let this idea sink in to the emotionally walled-off, vulnerable part of him, he was eventually able to see that this was probably true. But just gaining this insight wasn't enough to change things.

Step Three for Danny was to train himself to stop fleeing the closeness he felt when he and Roxy spent more time together. As they shared more and more of their emotional lives and deepened their interdependence, he continued to panic. But he practiced staying steady, talking with Roxy about what he was feeling when it was happening, using his support network, and even going to a therapist for a while to talk about his unresolved grief. Although none of this was easy, Danny was eventually able to open himself enough to settle in with Roxy. They now are the proud parents of two little boys and are enjoying their parenthood.

The Distracted Distancer: Changing Your Priorities

Now it's your turn to experience transformation. What do you need to do if you are in a relationship but completely absorbed in your children, work, friends, or community service? What if your involvement is an addiction that has kept you distracted from your partner?

Now that you are ready to make a change in your intimate relationship, here are some suggestions for you:

- Decide which activities you can cut back on or give up completely in order to prioritize your relationship. Be realistic. Don't choose to give up something completely that you can't possibly eliminate entirely.

- When you make the choice to cut back or give up something, that is, giving up your need to do whatever, work at it gradually. Take into account that letting go of anything, whether it's an addiction, stepping away from center stage in relation to your friends' lives, or being less consumed by the details of your children's lives, will take a lot of your time initially. You won't become an available partner overnight.

- Talk to your partner about the changes that may be necessary to make in the life you've been sharing up until now. Maybe your partner will have to take on more of the family-based tasks. Maybe you'll need to change aspects of your work life, and bring in less income. Maybe your withdrawal from activities outside your life and commitments as a couple will create some entirely new issues for the two of you to deal with.

- Schedule some regular one-on-one time with your partner, and stick to that commitment. To do this successfully, you'll need to be realistic about when this takes place and how much time you can commit to spending with your partner.

Don't start by planning to spend the whole twenty-four hours together every Saturday. That would be a setup for failure.

- Choose activities and settings for your couple time that will be mutually appealing and not too stressful. For example, it would be a mistake to commit to going out to clubs every week if you don't really enjoy the club scene. Find something you both feel comfortable doing. You could make a plan to spend Saturday nights together but leave the activity options open, thus allowing for enough variety to give the two of you varied opportunities to feel more connected.

- Take some risks engaging with your partner in quieter, more inward time together. This could mean talking about what's going on with you over a quiet meal or during a walk. It could involve some quiet time outdoors just enjoying the view, or spending some time together in meditation or prayer. Notice whether you're still trying to escape your emotions, fears, and memories.

- Check in to see how your partner is doing with the "new" you. How does he or she feel about you in this new stage of intimacy? How does your partner feel about him- or herself? Don't be surprised or discouraged if your partner becomes uncomfortable for a while. Maybe your partner has his or her own distancing tactics and this new couple closeness stirs up some discomfort for both of you.

Sally's Story

You may remember that Sally was able to turn things around in her marriage by changing her relationships with her siblings. She and Howard were now facing each other, both committed to deepening their relationship. At first, Sally was a wreck! She found every excuse in the book to avoid intimate time alone with her husband, including a series of minor illnesses, headaches, and bad moods.

But finally she recognized what she had been doing, and she began to implement the suggestions outlined above.

Once Sally and Howard talked over finding the time to plan a couple of activities, it actually wasn't so hard to figure out what to do. They went back to their courtship days, remembering how much they had both loved buying and sprucing up old furniture, quilts, kitchenware, and decorative objects. They decided to schedule a regular date to go out every Saturday searching for "treasures," to enjoy the excitement of finding them, and then to work together to clean up and evaluate their purchases.

It was great for Sally to see how smart and competent Howard was. This lessened her fearful view of him as a needy invalid. They also began to be playful with each other again, which brought back good memories of their earlier years together.

Occasionally, Sally would begin slipping back into her old distancer patterns, rushing to attend to her siblings, friends, and children when they were in a crisis. When this happened, Howard was able to gently help her notice what she was doing and more importantly to help her delegate some responsibilities to others.

They were thrilled when one of their new purchases, an old rocking chair, made them one-minute stars on the PBS Antiques Roadshow *program when it came to their part of New England. But even more thrilling was the comfort they were celebrating in their newly achieved closeness as a couple.*

Charting Your Progress

No matter what kind of distancer you are, you will need to keep track of how you're doing in a systematic way. This is to help you notice both the setbacks and successes. You should keep on writing what you discover about yourself in your journal. You will need to keep your support people in the loop so they can help you see anything that your inevitable blind spots may hide. Remember to keep on tuning in to see what your body tells you as you chug along toward your goals. You can also keep track of your progress by using the following exercise periodically over the weeks and months of your new venture.

Exercise

Your Intimacy Barometer

Use this scale:

1 = This doesn't describe me at all.
2 = This describes my behavior a little bit.
3 = This describes my behavior in some ways.
4 = This describes quite a lot of my behavior.
5 = This is definitely me!

Rate yourself from 1 to 5 to answer the following statements:

1. I am aware of it when I use old distancing tactics. ______
2. I am able to stop myself when I begin to use old distancing tactics. ______
3. I am being less judgmental toward others and myself. ______
4. I talk to my partner (or "date") about my fear of being hurt or rejected. ______
5. I talk to my partner (or "date") about my fear of getting in too deep and having to become the caretaker in the relationship. ______
6. I am prioritizing quality couple time every week. ______
7. I am talking to my support people about my new experiences and getting their feedback. ______
8. I am making notes in my journal every week. ______
9. I am practicing my new skills to help me get through my anxiety and fear. ______
10. I am able to see the humor in my adventures, especially when things don't go the way I thought they would. ______

11. I am learning to let go of trying to control everything.
12. I am feeling less lonely.
13. I am feeling more loving.
14. I am finding more ways to really enjoy couple time.
15. I am liking myself more than I used to.

The goal is to keep increasing your score. Don't expect to get to 75 right away. Do keep on working to encourage yourself, even when you think your score should be higher than it is. And if you're feeling brave, you might want to invite your partner to rate him- or herself, and then rate you. It will be interesting to share this exercise, to see if it helps you deepen your relationship even more.

Warning: If you are just now beginning to see someone new, doing this exercise together might be a little overwhelming. But you can use it to bring up some relationship issues you might want to talk over with this new person.

Ending the Story

Your story is just beginning, with many chapters left to write. But here's a quick summary of what happened to the other distancers who have been your companions and role models throughout this book.

Danny married Roxy and had two kids, as you know. You also know now that Sally and Howard revived the joys of their marriage by spending regular time together doing things that revitalized their delight in each other. You also found out that Jack met Celia, and they were able to work out a very happy relationship, one that allowed each to maintain a relatively high degree of separate time and space, but also provided great couple comfort and companionship. And Janine progressed from being a recluse to getting into a couple relationship with Wyatt. She also became a powerful advocate for women who had been victims of violence.

Luisa and Diego went their separate ways. Luisa eventually went to a therapist to talk about the feelings of shame and self-doubt that she had projected onto Diego. She met a man whose wife had left him, and they were able to share their stories of hurt and rejection and went on to get married to each other. They found pastoral counseling very helpful.

Diego decided to remain single. He continues to date a variety of women, and he is very mindful of not setting himself up by wanting too much from a partner. He is quite content for the time being to get his emotional needs met by friendships in his social activism groups.

Rick and his wife Carla have changed their relationship significantly as Rick learns to let go of trying to control everyone and everything. Carla is much happier now that she feels more competent in the marriage. They are experimenting with new ways to have fun together with their kids, and both report that their sexual relationship has become much more playful and much more satisfying.

Yvonne continues to experience ups and downs in regard to her sexual openness and comfort, but she is able to enjoy sex much more than she had ever expected to. As she and her boyfriend have moved beyond their original sexual impasse, she has discovered other areas in which she distances. She feels a new awareness of how afraid she is of giving in to her own desires, wishes, preferences, and dreams. She has just decided to go back to school to study marine biology. To do this, she is ready to relocate to another part of the country if necessary, and her boyfriend is willing to move with her, but only if she wants him to.

Colin got very involved in Alcoholics Anonymous where he met a woman who had been sober for quite a long time. They went out in groups after the meetings for a while, and then began dating. Colin reverted to his old fear-based distancing pattern of using a lot of sarcastic humor, and, predictably, his new friend broke off the relationship. Slowly, Colin began to see what was happening and began really talking to her about himself when they briefly chatted after the AA meetings. Eventually, he regained her trust and they got back together. It remains to be seen whether they will stay together, but the prognosis is good.

Andrew met a recently divorced young woman with a young child. He has been able to show up for both the woman and her child. He is cautiously in love. He has learned to stick to a very strict schedule of physical exercise—running and strength training—to contain his hyperactivity, and he is happier than he's ever been.

Ben is still single, although he is more comfortable with himself than he was before. Lately, he's been considering a radical lifestyle change that would involve moving to India to live in a spiritual community where the residents are committed to community but remain single and celibate.

Now It's Your Turn

You are now writing your own story. Make it as full of courage, new adventures, and happiness as you can. You know everything you need to know and you have the skills to do it. It's up to you. You can do it, just as long as you keep your expectations reasonable. Keep on learning to like yourself and your own company. The more you trust and like yourself, the more others will feel the same way. Go for it!

References

Bly, Robert. 1990. *Iron John: A Book About Men*. New York: Addison-Wesley.

Chödrön, Pema. 2002. *Comfortable with Uncertainty*. Boston: Shambhala Publications.

Gray, John. 1992. *Men Are from Mars, Women Are from Venus*. New York: HarperCollins.

Real, Terrence. 2002. *How Can I Get Through to You? Closing the Intimacy Gap Between Men and Women*. New York: Simon & Schuster, Fireside Books.

Dusty Miller, Ed.D., is a clinical psychologist, writer, trainer, and internationally-recognized expert in the areas of trauma, addiction, and self-sabotage—including relationship self-sabotage such as distancing. She is the director of the ATRIUM Institute in Northampton, MA. Miller offers training, consultation, and workshops for professionals and paraprofessionals who work with traumatic stress, substance abuse, relational challenges, and more. She is author of Women Who Hurt Themselves, Addictions and Trauma Recovery, and Your Surviving Spirit.